Hardening Cisco Routers

Hardening Cisco Routers

Thomas Akin

O'REILLY®

Beijing · Cambridge · Farnham · Köln · Paris · Sebastopol · Taipei · Tokyo

Hardening Cisco Routers
by Thomas Akin

Copyright © 2002 O'Reilly Media, Inc., Inc. All rights reserved.
Printed in the United States of America.

Published by O'Reilly Media, Inc., 1005 Gravenstein Highway North,
Sebastopol, CA 95472.

O'Reilly Media, Inc. books may be purchased for educational, business, or sales promotional use. On-line editions are also available for most titles (*safari.oreilly.com*). For more information, contact our corporate/institutional sales department: (800) 998-9938 or *corporate@oreilly.com*.

Editor:	Jim Sumser
Production Editor:	Ann Schirmer
Cover Designer:	Emma Colby
Interior Designer:	Melanie Wang

Printing History:

February 2002:	First Edition.

RepKover™ This book uses RepKover™, a durable and flexible lay-flat binding.

ISBN: 0-596-00166-5
[M]   [3/05]LCP

Table of Contents

Preface

Master one single topic, and everything becomes clearer.

The field of network security is a huge subject. To be a network security expert, you must be an expert on routers, switches, hubs, firewalls, intrusion detection systems (IDS), servers, desktops, email, HTTP, instant messages, sniffers, and a thousand other topics. There are many books on network security, and the good ones tend to be tomes of 1000+ pages that are intimidating even to their authors. This book takes the opposite approach. It takes a single, but vitally important, topic and expands on it. Routers are your first line of defense. If they are compromised, everything else is compromised. This book describes how to secure your routers. Once you learn how to secure them, routers can protect the rest of your network.

To reemphasize, this is not a book on network security; there are hundreds of those already in print. You will not find long discussions on firewalls, Virtual Private Networks (VPNs), network IDS systems, or even access lists (ACLs). This book is more fundamental than that. This book shows how to harden the foundation of your network—the router. Once you have mastered the information in this book, you will find that your ability to build firewalls and configure IDS systems will increase. You will be building on a secure foundation.

Organization

This book consists of 11 chapters and 5 appendixes. At the end of most chapters is a checklist summarizing the hardening techniques described in that chapter. Appendix A provides a complete hardening checklist made up of the chapter checklists. The book is designed to be read either straight through for those new to router security, or a chapter at a time for those interested in specific topics. I recommend, however, that before reading the book, you review the checklist provided in Appendix A. This checklist will give you a good feel for the information covered in each chapter and familiarize you with the scope of the book. Here is a brief description of what each chapter and appendix covers.

Chapter 1, *Router Security*, addresses the importance of router security and where routers fit into an overall information security plan. Additionally, this chapter discusses which routers are the most important to secure and how secure routers are necessary (and often overlooked) parts of both firewall design and the overall information security strategy of a company.

Chapter 2, *IOS Version Security*, discusses security issues involving the router IOS software. It outlines current IOS revisions, shows how to determine current IOS versions, and details the importance of running a current IOS.

Chapter 3, *Basic Access Control*, discusses the standard ways to access a Cisco router, the security implications of each of these methods, and how to secure basic Cisco router access. These methods include console, VTY, AUX, and HTTP access controls.

Chapter 4, *Passwords and Privilege Levels*, discusses the three ways that Cisco routers store passwords and the security implications of each method. This chapter continues to discuss the router's default security levels and shows how to modify these levels to increase the security and accountability on your routers.

Chapter 5, *AAA Access Control*, discusses how to use the advanced AAA authentication and authorization configuration for Cisco routers. It also shows how to use a network access server running RADIUS or TACACS+ to control these services on the router.

Chapter 6, *Warning Banners*, discusses the importance of having warning banners on routers. This chapter not only talks about the need to have banners, but also presents legal dos and don'ts for security banners. Finally, the chapter provides an example recommended banner to use on Cisco routers.

Chapter 7, *Unnecessary Protocols and Services*, discusses the unnecessary services that are commonly run on Cisco routers. Many of these services are enabled by default, and this chapter explains why services such as HTTP, *finger*, CDP, *echo*, and *chargen* are dangerous and details how to turn them off.

Chapter 8, *SNMP Security*, demonstrates how to disable SNMP or configure it securely. It presents the differences between SNMP Versions 1, 2, and 3; talks about read-only versus read-write access; and shows how to use access lists to limit SNMP access to only a few specific machines.

Chapter 9, *Secure Routing and Antispoofing*, discusses routing protocol security. Specifically, it discusses how to add security to RIP, OSPF, EIGRP, and BGP. These routing protocols allow authentication to prevent fake routing updates. The chapter also presents the importance of antispoofing filters and how to perform ingress and egress filtering using CLs on older routers and Cisco's RPF and CEF antispoofing mechanisms on newer ones.

Chapter 10, *NTP*, discusses NTP and how to use it to make sure all routers have the exact same time. This chapter discusses the importance of having the time on all your routers and logging servers synchronized and provides examples of how to configure a Cisco router to use NTP time services.

Chapter 11, *Logging*, discusses how Cisco routers perform logging and why logging is important. The chapter then demonstrates why and how to manipulate logging buffers, how to configure routers to use *syslog*, and when to do ACL violation logging.

Appendix A, *Checklist Quick Reference*, allows you to secure your Cisco routers and verify that important security issues have been addressed. The checklist is presented in a manner that makes it easy to quickly refer back to the chapter addressing the items outlined in the checklist reference. Finally, this appendix briefly talks about using the checklist to harden and audit Cisco routers.

Appendix B, *Physical Security*, talks about the importance of physically securing your routers. It presents common physical vulnerabilities and discusses how to overcome them.

Appendix C, *Incident Response*, gets you thinking about how to react when a break-in is discovered. The goal of this chapter is not to provide an exhaustive explanation of incident response, but to provide emergency guidelines that you can follow when an incident occurs.

Appendix D, *Configuration Examples*, provides common Cisco router configuration examples that combine the examples throughout the book.

Appendix E, *Resources*, provides a list of resources that you might find useful if you need to brush up on ACLs, network access protocols such as TACACS or RADIUS, and services such as SNMP or *syslog*.

Audience

This book assumes you are already familiar with configuring, administering, and troubleshooting Cisco routers. A CCNA should be comfortable with the contents of each chapter. A CCNP or above will probably want to first turn to the checklist provided in Appendix A. To get the most out of this book, you should be familiar with:

- Accessing your router through the console and VTYs
- Using TCP/IP and subnet masks
- Configuring your router from the command line
- Upgrading your IOS
- Configuring standard and extended ACLs
- Routing protocols such as RIP, IGRP, and OSPF

Conventions Used in This Book

The following formatting conventions are used throughout this book:

- *Italic* is used for commands, passwords, error messages, filenames, emphasis, and the first use of technical terms.
- Constant width is used for IP addresses and router configuration examples.
- *Constant width italic* is used for replaceable text.
- **Constant width bold** is used for user input.

 This icon indicates a note or tip.

 This icon indicates a warning.

How to Contact Us

Please address comments and questions concerning this book to the publisher:

O'Reilly & Associates, Inc.
1005 Gravenstein Highway North
Sebastopol, CA 95472
(800) 998-9938 (in the United States or Canada)
(707) 829-0515 (international/local)
(707) 829-0104 (fax)

There is a web site for this book, which lists errata, examples, or any additional information. You can access this page at:

http://www.oreilly.com/catalog/hardcisco

To comment or ask technical questions about this book, send email to:

bookquestions@oreilly.com

For more information about books, conferences, resource centers, and the O'Reilly Network, see the O'Reilly web site at:

http://www.oreilly.com

Acknowledgments

First, always, is my wife Abigail Akin. Neither of us knew how hard this would be, but it was her encouragement (and occasional kick in the pants) that gave me the courage and discipline to write and finish this book. Honey, this first book is for you.

Second, for his near infinite patience, is Jim Sumser, my editor. It was Jim who took a chance on an unknown author. He pushed me when I needed it and always had a word of praise to keep me on track just when I was about to throw my computer out the window.

My technical reviewers gave invaluable input: Ian J. Brown, CCIE #3372, Mark Jackson, CCIE #4736, and Elsa Lankford. Ian and Mark kept me towing the line technically, while Elsa kept me from getting bogged down in details, missing the forest for the trees. Ian and Mark, the configuration examples in Appendix D are for you, and, Elsa, the resources in Appendix E are yours.

Also, my friends in law enforcement: thanks to Steve Edwards from the Georgia Bureau of Investigation and Cassandra Schansman, Georgia's Assistant Attorney General, for both their support and review of Appendix C. Thanks to Patrick Gray from the FBI's Atlanta Computer Crimes Squad for providing the warning banner in Chapter 6.

Next, Jeff Crabtree, my former boss and long-time friend. He gave me my start in information technology and has supported me, many times at his own expense, for almost a decade. I owe you and Lisa some serious margaritas.

Finally, the two people who have taught me that integrity and love are the most important parts of being successful—my father Morgan Akin and my mother Cathy Coulmas.

CHAPTER 1

Router Security

In Webster's dictionary the definition of *hard* is particularly relevant to the field of information security:

> Not easily penetrated or separated into parts; not yielding to pressure.

By hardening a router, we make it difficult to penetrate and unyielding under the pressure of attacks. This chapter discusses why hardening network routers is one of the most important and overlooked aspects of Information Security. It will talk about what can go wrong when routers are left insecure and identify which routers are at the most risk from attack.

Router Security?

When asking about Information Security (InfoSec), most people immediately think about stolen credit cards, defaced web sites, and teenage hackers with names like *B@D@pple*. An InfoSec professional might extend the list to items like firewalls, Virtual Private Networks (VPN)s, penetration testing, and risk analysis. What is almost never listed is router security—network security, yes, but never specifically router security. The distinction is important.

Network security is most often thought of as something that protects machines on a network. To do this, companies put up firewalls, configure VPNs, and install intrusion detection systems. Router security, however, involves protecting the network itself by hardening or securing the routers. Specifically, it addresses preventing attackers from:

- Using routers to gain information about your network for use in an attack (information leakage)
- Disabling your routers (and therefore your network)
- Reconfiguring your routers
- Using your routers to launch further internal attacks
- Using your routers to launch further external attacks

Organizations spend hundreds of thousands of dollars on firewalls, VPNs, intrusion detection, and other security measures, and yet they run routers with out-of-the-box configurations. From personal experience, at least eight or nine out of every ten networks has routers that are vulnerable to one of the five preceding problems.

Routers: The Foundation of the Internet

A layperson who is asked what the foundation of the Internet is will probably say the World Wide Web, with the explanation that it is what everyone uses. Ask an MCSE and you may get a claim about how everyone runs Windows. Ask a network engineer and you will get routers and the statement "nothing works without them." Without routers there is no Web, no email, no Internet.

The fundamental piece of information on the Internet is the IP packet. A router's primary function is to direct these packets. Therefore, routers truly work at the most basic and fundamental level of the Internet. Every network attached to the Internet is attached by a router. Some may be Linux boxes acting as routers, others may be firewalls also performing routing, but most will be dedicated Cisco routers. Current estimates indicate that 80 percent of the Internet runs on Cisco equipment.

Routers are not only the foundation of the Internet; they are the foundation of how your company communicates both externally and internally. Additionally, there is a strong trend toward converging voice, data, and even video into a single network running IP. With this push, routers are becoming the foundation of data, voice, and video communication. With this convergence, almost all of a company's information will pass through routers, causing them to become extremely attractive targets.

What Can Go Wrong

Efforts to improve awareness about the importance of router security are not helped by the lack of media attention on incidents involving compromised routers. Why the lack of reported cases? There are two major reasons:

- Routers are often used to provide attackers with valuable information about your network and servers rather than being the object of direct attack themselves.
- Router compromises are much less likely to be detected.

Before any attack, hackers will gather as much information about a company, its network, and its servers as possible. The more information an attacker can get, the easier it is to compromise a site—knowledge is power. This type of information gathering is called *footprinting,* and routers are routinely used when footprinting a site. With default configurations, an attacker can query routers and map out entire networks, including subnets, addressing schemes, and redundant paths. With this information, an attacker can determine the most vulnerable locations on the network. Footprinting a site, however, is a tedious and unglamorous process. The media reports that it took a hacker 15 minutes to break into NASA; they don't point out that the hacker spent 6 weeks gathering information before launching the attack.

Making matters worse, few organization have any controls or monitoring on their routers. When asked, "How would you know if someone reconfigured your router?" the answer invariably comes back, "When it stops working." Prodding further with a question about how to detect changes that kept the network functional but allowed an attacker to bypass a firewall usually gets a comment about how the intrusion detection system (IDS) would catch them. Pointing out that if a router were compromised, attackers could probably bypass the IDS finally induces concern. With the current lack of controls and auditing on routers, compromises will probably go unnoticed unless they disrupt service. Attacks that disrupt service are bad, but at least companies know something is wrong—they know they have been hacked. Attacks in which a hacker does disable anything are the truly dangerous ones. Without adequate monitoring and auditing, no one knows the network has been compromised. An attacker can spend weeks or months monitoring all network traffic, gaining bank account numbers, client lists, or personnel records. This information could be sold to competitors, given to other hackers, or used to blackmail the company.

Consequences of Compromised Routers

In modern warfare, a key strategy to attack an enemy's ability to communicate. The obvious attack disables an enemy's ability to communicate. A subtler attack compromises, but does not disable, an enemy's communications system. This type of compromise allows easy access to enemy plans, troop movement, and points of attack. The compromise also allows false information to be transmitted to the enemy, confusing them and leading them into traps.

All networked organizations are in a battle to protect their resources and information. Secure communication is as important for an organization's survival as it is in military warfare. Routers are the communication medium for an organization and the consequences of their compromise can be disastrous. By compromising an organization's routers, an attacker can:

Disable the entire network
> Those who have experienced significant network outages can understand the loss of productivity and revenue this causes. Imagine how long it would take to fix the network if attackers disabled password recovery, changed the routers' passwords, and deleted the configurations.

Use the routers to attack internal systems
> Routers can give attackers a foothold into your internal network. By taking control of routers, attackers can often bypass intrusion detection systems, use the routers to gain access to trusted networks, and avoid or confuse any logging and monitoring used on the network.

Use the routers to attack other sites

Hackers like to hide their tracks. They do this by breaking into several networked systems and use those systems to launch other attacks. When attacks pass through six or seven servers, they can be hard to trace. Since routers usually have less protection and logging than servers, attacking through six or seven routers can be extremely difficult and costly to investigate. For organizations with insecure routers and no monitoring, an attacker will leave little or no trace.

Reroute all traffic entering and leaving the network

Compromised routers allow an attacker to reroute network traffic. Attackers can then monitor, record, and modify the redirected traffic. Imagine the effects of several weeks worth of online orders being redirected to a competitor or, worse, online financial transactions being rerouted to a bank somewhere in Nigeria.

What Routers Are at Risk?

A simple, but useful, risk analysis formula defines risk as:

$$\text{Risk} = \text{vulnerability} \times \text{threat} \times \text{cost}$$

where vulnerability is how likely an attack is to succeed, threat is the likelihood of an attack, and cost is the total cost of a threat succeeding.

The link between threat and vulnerability can be confusing but is important to understand. If a high-rise office building is designed and built without any protection against earthquakes, then the office building has a vulnerability to earthquakes. The vulnerability alone, though, does not necessarily translate into risk for the people working in the office building. If the building is located in California, there is a significant threat of earthquakes, so a vulnerable building provides a great amount of risk. The same building located in Georgia, while being equally vulnerable to earthquakes, would have a lower risk since the threat of earthquakes in Georgia is much lower.

When evaluating routers, the vulnerability usually averages around the same level. Even though different routers may run different IOS versions, routers inherently trust other routers. They trust one another in order to exchange routing information, allowing them to correctly transfer packets and route around problems. Once a single router is compromised, this trust can be exploited to manipulate other routers on a network. For this reason, it is advantageous to assume that all routerrs on the network share the same level of vulnerability. This level should be equal to the vulnerability of the most vulnerable router on the network.

With the vulnerability equal, the differentiating factors become threat and cost. The threat to external routers is generally greater due to their visibility. Other routers may provide access to secured or trusted networks, and their compromise would cost much more than a router connected to a public lab or test area.

With these considerations in mind, some of the first routers that need to be secured and actively monitored are:

- Gateway routers that connect your network to the Internet
- Routers that are part of a firewall
- Routers that are connected to a trusted or secure network
- Routers that perform packet filtering

Moving Forward

This chapter has explained what router security is and why it is vitally important. Routers provide one of the most fundamental functions on a network and are often installed and run with out-of-the-box security. When addressing router security, most administrators think about using access lists to turn off *ping* or Telnet. Digging further and asking about the specific measures taken to protect the routers themselves usually results in a blank stare or a statement such as, "Our routers don't hold any critical data, and we have never had any security problems with them, so they must be secure." The "we have never had any problems with them" argument sounds very powerful, especially to management and those who hold the purse strings. This chapter provides insight into why this is such a dangerous view.

The rest of this book discusses what it takes to harden a Cisco router; Appendix A provides a checklist that summarizes the steps necessary to harden a router and protect the network.

CHAPTER 2

IOS Version Security

The first item to discuss when talking about router security is the router's operating system (OS). The OS on Cisco routers is called Internetworking Operating System, or IOS. Most routers will be running an IOS version between 11.x and 12.x. By the time this book is published, Cisco may have released 13.x. Every OS has vulnerabilities, and IOS is no exception. These vulnerabilities generally allow an attacker to disable a router (a denial of service attack), collect information from a router (information leakage), or reconfigure a router (an actual compromise).

The Need for a Current IOS

A key aspect of every good security plan involves operating system security. Every operating system connected to the Internet is subject to attack. Hackers look for OS vulnerabilities to exploit. Cisco IOS has come under increasing scrutiny over the past few years. *Bugtraq*, a full disclosure vulnerability forum, reports 14 Cisco vulnerabilities between 1992 and 1999, 23 in 2000, and 42 in 2001. Once posted on *Bugtraq*, these vulnerabilities are seen by thousands of hackers a day and are used in numerous attacks. With such an increase in vulnerabilities, secure routers must have a current and stable version of IOS. The next section on IOS versions provides information on how to identify secure IOS releases.

Determining the IOS Version

You must know what IOS version your routers are currently running before determining whether you should use the latest release. To determine the IOS version, log into your router and type **show version**. The output will be similar to:

```
Cisco Internetwork Operating System Software IOS(tm)
GS Software (RSP-P-MZ), Version 12.0(16), RELEASE SOFTWARE (fc1)
Copyright (c) 1986-1999 by Cisco Systems, Inc.
Compiled Wed 06-Jan-99 08:15 by preetha
```

The author has highlighted the important IOS information. The first is Version 12. 0(16), showing the IOS release version. This is followed by text indicating the release type. For the sake of security and stability, this text should normally read RELEASE SOFTWARE. If it reads anything else, such as EARLY DEPLOYMENT RELEASE SOFTWARE or MAINTENANCE INTERIM SOFTWARE, the router is not running one of the most stable and secure releases.

IOS Versions and Vulnerabilities

Once you know what IOS version your routers are running, you need to understand the IOS release process. Without this understanding, identifying and choosing the most secure release can be very difficult.

IOS Versions

Cisco has a very defined and often confusing procedure for releasing IOS versions. There are two major types of IOS releases:

Early Deployment
> Early Deployment (ED) releases are used to add features to Cisco's IOS. These releases contain feature and platform support that has not yet been tested extensively in production systems. It is relatively easy for Cisco to add additional features or platform support to ED releases, but these additions have had very little testing in production environments.

Major Release
> The goal of Major Releases is stability and quality. Major Releases provide images for all Cisco hardware and once a release become a Major Release, no additional features or platforms added. The only changes to these releases are in the form of bug fixes.

Both Early Deployment and Major Releases are broken down into subcategories. Early Deployment releases are broken down into four types:

Consolidated Technology Early Deployment (CTED)
> Cisco uses the CTED to add enhancements, new features, and new hardware platforms to the IOS. These releases are extremely feature rich, but at the cost of stability and reliability.

Specific Technology Early Deployment (STED)
> STED releases are similar to CTED releases, but are targeted toward a specific technology and are always released on specific platforms.

Specific Market Early Deployment (SMED)
> These releases target specific market segments such as ISPs or financial institutions. Unlike STED releases, which are organized according to technology,

SMED releases are organized around a specific market segment. These releases are built only for the specific platforms needed by the target market.

X Releases

X Releases are short-lived, one-time releases. These releases exist to allow Cisco to add new features and platforms to a CTED release in an extremely short period of time in order to get these enhancements to market quickly. After successful testing, X Releases are ported back into the CTED releases immediately.

Major Releases can be broken down into two subcategories:

Limited Deployment

Limited Deployment (LD) releases are the first official Major Releases of IOS code. They have passed through the Early Deployment phase and include many of the new features and product support developed under the ED releases. Once a release is in the LD phase, no additional features, platforms, or enhancements can be made to the release—only bug fixes. Limited Deployment releases, however, have not yet been extensively tested in actual production networks.

General Deployment

After 9 to 14 months of testing in Limited Deployment, IOS versions enter General Deployment (GD). Once an IOS version reaches this phase, there are strict controls over any modifications to the code. The goal for GD releases is to remain as stable as possible. Not all releases reach General Deployment (for example, 11.1 and 11.3).

One more type of release needs to be mentioned: a Deferred Release (DF). These releases are designated by DF and occur when Cisco cancels and makes obsolete a release somewhere in the cycle. Releases are usually deferred because of significant quality issues and should be avoided.

From a security standpoint, organizations should normally be running GD releases. These releases are the most stable and have the most testing behind them. Other releases should be run only if an organization requires the additional functionality provided by another release and if a risk analysis indicates that they can handle the instability and insecurity often associated with the other releases.

Please note that, not knowing any better, many organizations run ED and LD releases and often have no problems. Cisco's release process is done very well, and even these releases are generally stable and secure. However, the field of security requires one to be a little paranoid and, unless there are significant reasons to run other releases, the best practice is to stick with GD releases.

Finally, while running a General Deployment release should keep you safe from currently known problems and vulnerabilities, don't let the GD release lull you into a false sense of confidence. Vulnerabilities are still discovered in GD releases, so it is extremely important to monitor the status of your releases to make sure new bugs have not been uncovered.

IOS Naming Scheme

In addition to the release system, choosing the right IOS release requires an understanding of Cisco's naming conventions. The first is the Major Release number. Examples of Major Release numbers are 12.1, 12.0, 11.3, 11.2, and 11.1. Bug fixes to Major Releases are included in maintenance revisions released every eight weeks. The number inside the parentheses indicates maintenance revisions. For example, 12.0(3) indicates Major Release 12.0 and maintenance revision 3.

Limited or General Deployment releases consist of only Major Release and maintenance revision numbers. While the first few maintenance releases are going to be LD releases, there is no way to determine from the IOS number whether a release is in Limited or General Deployment. To find out, go to *http://www.cisco.com* and choose Products → Cisco IOS Software → Key Release Dates and Milestones, where the GD release dates are listed.

Identifying Early Deployment releases is easier. Letters or groups of letters are always assigned to ED releases:

CTED

> The feature-rich Consolidated Technology releases can be identified by a T appended after the release number—12.0T , 12.1(3)T, or 11.3(15)T.

STED

> The Specific Technology releases can be identified by two letters (excluding X) appended after the release number—11.1CA, 11.3(12)MA, or 12.0(3)NB. The first letter is used to specify the technology (see Table 2-1) and the second is used for differentiation.

SMED

> The Specific Market releases can be identified by a single letter after the release number (except for a T, which indicates a CTED release.) Examples of SMED releases are 12.1E or 12.0(14)S.

X Releases

> These one-time releases can be identified by two letters—an X followed by a letter for differentiation.

The following letters help identify ED releases. These definitions apply when the letters are in the *first position* after the IOS release name.

Table 2-1. First letter of ED releases

Letter	Meaning
A	Access server/dial technology
D	xDSL technology
E	Enterprise feature set
H	SDH/SONET technology

Table 2-1. First letter of ED releases (continued)

Letter	Meaning
N	Voice, multimedia, conference
S	Service provider
T	Consolidated Technology (CTED)
W	ATM/LAN switching/layer 3 switching
X	One-time release based on a CTED release

An X or Y in the second position indicates a short-lived Early Deployment release based on a Specific Technology (STED) release. For example, 11.3NX is based on 11.3 NA and 12.0(3)WX is based on 12.0(3)WA.

Finally, in the case of a major bug, Cisco may fix and rebuild an IOS release. To differentiate these rebuilds from the original release, Cisco appends a number or letter to the end of the release number. If the release ends in a letter, Cisco appends a number. If the release ends in a number, Cisco appends a letter. If 12.0(3)T was rebuilt, the number would be 12.0(3)T1. A rebuild of 11.3(13) would yield 11.3(13a) and a rebuild of 12.1(2)NA would result in 12.1(2)NA1.

Vulnerabilities

To determine which versions of IOS have vulnerabilities, go to *http://www.cisco. com/go/psirt* to find the latest security information. Unfortunately, Cisco provides no summary of vulnerable IOS versions, and determining your vulnerability requires going through most Security Advisories individually. With the numerous IOS versions available, choosing a General Deployment makes checking for security vulnerabilities easier.

IOS Security Checklist

This checklist summarizes the important security information presented in this chapter. A complete security checklist is provided in Appendix A.

- Make sure that all routers are running a current IOS.
- Make sure that the IOS version is in General Deployment (unless all risks with the non-GD IOS version have been addressed).
- Check the IOS version against existing Cisco Security Advisories.
- Regularly check Cisco Security Advisories for IOS vulnerabilities.

CHAPTER 3

Basic Access Control

This chapter addresses what most people think about when they start to secure a router—authenticating users and restricting access. There are many more ways to access Cisco routers than most network administrators realize. Each of these methods can have different authentication methods and can be set to allow various levels of privilege access. It is important that all methods of access are either secured or disabled. The chapter briefly discusses the differences between authentication and authorization and then moves on to the fundamentals of how Cisco routers handle controlling and protecting access.

Authentication Versus Authorization

Access control involves both authentication and authorization. People often confuse the two. Authentication is the process of identifying a user; authorization restricts what a user is allowed to do. Cisco router authentication controls can be divided into two main categories—those that use the AAA (authentication, authorization, accounting) access methods and those that don't. The non-AAA methods include line authentication (console, auxiliary, and VTY ports), local username authentication, and Terminal Access Controller Access Control System (TACACS) or extended TACACS authentication. The AAA authentication methods add TACACS+, RADIUS, and Kerberos. AAA provides much greater control over authentication, authorization, and accounting than do non-AAA methods. While Cisco calls AAA the primary and recommended method of access control, you must configure AAA on your router manually. This chapter describes non-AAA methods of access. AAA will be discussed in Chapter 5.

Points of Access

There are many ways to access a Cisco router. Each way can provide different levels of authorization, from viewing router information to completely reconfiguring the router or some level in between. Each access method is either out-of-band, which does not rely on the network, or in-band, which requires the network to be functional. The primary methods of access are through the console port, the auxiliary port, or network access through virtual TTYs (VTYs), HTTP, TFTP, or SNMP. The first three—console, auxiliary, and VTYs—are called *lines*. Each of the six methods has different characteristics.

Console port

The console port is the main access point on Cisco routers. It is the only one enabled by default and it requires physical access to the router. The console port has special abilities not associated with the other methods of access (such as performing password recovery in the event that a router is misconfigured or passwords are forgotten).

The console port is the only port that is automatically authorized to perform the special function of password recovery. If an organization loses all passwords to a router or if a router is compromised and reconfigured, there must to be a way to access the router without a password. Password recovery allows an administrator to access the router and delete or change the current passwords. Regarding password recovery, the only method of authentication is physical access to the router—anyone with physical access to the router can perform password recovery. This makes physical security of the router vitally important. See Appendix B for a checklist on how to secure physical access to the router.

Auxiliary port

The auxiliary or AUX port is used to provide out-of-band access to the router by allowing a modem or terminal server to be attached to the router. This port allows remote administration of the router even if the network itself is disabled.

Virtual TTY

Virtual TTYs (VTYs) provide terminal access to the router through the network itself. To gain access through a VTY, the network must be up and functioning. The most common protocol used to access a VTY is Telnet, but many other protocols, such as *rlogin* and *ssh*, are supported. VTYs can even support non-IP protocols, such as MOP or X.29. Cisco routers come with five VTY ports numbered 0 through 4, configured by default.

HTTP

Recent Cisco IOS revisions have added the ability to access and even reconfigure routers though the Web. When enabled, routers run a small web server that authenticates the user and provides access.

TFTP

Routers use the Trivial File Transfer Protocol (TFTP) to upload IOS software and configuration files. TFTP access usually becomes a concern only when routers are set to automatically load their configuration files from a TFTP server or are configured to act as TFTP servers themselves.

SNMP

    The Simple Network Management Protocol (SNMP) provides read-only and read/write access to almost all network devices. This method of access is discussed in detail in Chapter 8.

Basic Access Control

By default, there are two levels of authorization on Cisco routers (level 1 and level 15), and both require separate authentication. Level 1 is equivalent to read-only access, and level 15 give privileged or read/write access. Level 1 authorization allows users to view information about the router (but not make any changes) and is generally referred to as *user mode*. Level 15 gives the user full rights to reconfigure the router and is referred to as *privileged mode*.

Authentication and Authorization

Default router access first requires an administrator to gain user-level access before attempting privileged-level access. Thus, protecting and controlling user-level access into the routers is a primary concern. The default methods for access are the lines—console port, auxiliary port, and virtual TTYs. Additional methods include HTTP, TFTP, and SNMP access, and each method of access requires its own access control configuration.

Console password

The console port is used for direct access to the router and must be configured for secure access. By default, the console port's authentication method is a password (no username) and its authorization level is user or read-only. To configure the console port password from privileged mode, you must:

- Enter global configuration mode with the *config terminal* command
- Enter the line console with the *line console 0* command
- Enable logins using the *login* command
- Establish a password with the *password* command

Here is an example:

```
Router#config terminal
Enter configuration commands, one per line.  End with CNTL/Z.
Router(config)#line console 0
Router(config-line)#login
Router(config-line)#password console-password
Router(config-line)#^Z
Router#
```

Never put a modem on a console port. With a little patience and a war dialer, attackers can use the console port to perform password recovery remotely over the modem.

AUX and VTY passwords

Setting passwords on AUX and VTY ports is similar to setting the console password. Setting the password on the AUX port looks like:

```
Router#config terminal
Enter configuration commands, one per line.  End with CNTL/Z.
Router(config)#line aux 0
Router(config-line)#login
Router(config-line)#password aux-password
Router(config-line)#^Z
Router#
```

Setting the VTY password is slightly different since there are five VTY ports by default. Setting the password for the first VTY (VTY 0) would look like:

```
Router#config terminal
Enter configuration commands, one per line.  End with CNTL/Z.
Router(config)#line vty 0
Router(config-line)#login
Router(config-line)#password vty0-password
Router(config-line)#^Z
Router#
```

Setting the VTY password for all five default VTYs at the same time would look like:

```
Router#config terminal
Enter configuration commands, one per line.  End with CNTL/Z.
Router(config)#line vty 0 4
Router(config-line)#login
Router(config-line)#password vty-password
Router(config-line)#^Z
Router#
```

If you have configured additional VTYs on your router, you must make sure that a password is configured on all of them.

After these commands, a *show running-config* shows:

```
line con 0
 password console-password
 login
line aux 0
 password aux-password
 login
line vty 0 4
 password vty-password
 login
```

Don't forget that any changes you make are not automatically saved. Changes appear in the running configuration only until they are saved with the command *copy running-config startup-config*. If you don't save your changes, they will disappear the next time the router is rebooted.

Privileged-level access control

Once a user is logged into a line with user-level access, he can use the *enable* command to attempt to gain privilege access. Privilege access allows a user to both view router information and reconfigure the router. If there is no privilege-level password set, then the *enable* command grants privileged-level access with prompting for a password.

There are two ways to set the enable password—with the *enable password* command and the *enable secret* command. The *enable password* command is provided for backward compatibility only, is much less secure than the *enable secret* command, and should never be used. See Chapter 4 for more details on password encryption, but always use the *enable secret* command to set the enable password:

```
Router#config terminal
Enter configuration commands, one per line.  End with CNTL/Z.
Router(config)#enable secret enable-password
Router(config)#^Z
Router#
```

Cisco routers can also use *tacacs* (see the later section "TACACS access control") for the enable password (or they can use the more advanced AAA methods detailed in Chapter 5).

The *enable secret* command takes precedence over the *enable password* command, so if both are set, the system will use only the password established by the *enable secret* command.

Local username access control

Default Cisco router authentication does not require a login name and has no concept of identity. This scales very poorly because when more than one administrator knows the router password, there is no accountability. Local authentication solves the accountability issue by letting users be defined on each router and each point of access configured to use locally defined usernames and passwords.

To use local authentication, first configure user accounts on each router and then configure each line to use these usernames for authentication. To create users, use the *username* command:

```
Router#config terminal
Enter configuration commands, one per line.  End with CNTL/Z.
Router(config)#username jdoe password jdoe-password
Router(config)#username rsmith password rsmith-password
```

```
Router(config)#^Z
Router#
```

Next, tell each line to use local authentication by using the *login local* command:

```
Router#config terminal
Enter configuration commands, one per line.  End with CNTL/Z.
Router(config)#line vty 0 4
Router(config-line)#login local
Router(config-line)#^Z
Router#
```

This example configured only the VTY ports; you should also configure the AUX and console ports to use local authentication.

Local authentication can solve our accountability problems, but it doesn't help with scalability. If a company has a dozen routers, every time an account needs to be created, deleted, or modified, the change must be made separately on all 12 routers. Local authentication also has the vulnerability of the passwords either being presented in clear text or with a reversible encryption (as explained in Chapter 4).

TACACS access control

The only basic, non-AAA access control setting that can help solve the scalability problems is TACACS. Cisco routers support three versions of TACACS—standard TACACS, Extended TACACS (X-TACACS), and TACACS Plus (TACACS+). The supported non-AAA versions are TACACS and X-TACACS.

TACACS can provide centralized access control on a network. Instead of each router being statically configured with all usernames and passwords, it is configured to ask a TACACS server for information about who is allowed to log in to the router. If you have a dozen routers and all are configured to use a TACACS server for authentication, the only list of usernames and passwords that need to be kept and updated is on the TACACS server.

TACACS and X-TACACS have been declared end-of-maintenance by Cisco, which means they can drop support for them at any time. Therefore, this chapter provides only a brief overview of a TACACS configuration. If you currently use one of these two protocols, you are encouraged to migrate to TACACS+, RADIUS, or Kerberos. All three continue to be supported by Cisco routers. If you want to establish a network access server to centralize your authentication, pretend that TACACS and XTACACS don't exist and read about TACACS+, RADIUS, and Kerberos in Chapter 5.

To be complete, however, look at the following examples of using a TACACS server to authenticate user access to a router. The basic steps are:

1. Configure each line to use TACACS with the *login tacacs* command.
2. Set the password of last resort to the enable password with the *tacacs-server last-resort password* command. In case the router cannot contact the TACACS server

for authentication information, it will not lock you out, but will allow you to log in using the privilege mode password.

3. Tell the router what TACACS server to use with the *tacacs-server host* command.

Here is an example of setting the AUX port to use the TACACS server 130.218.10.12 for authentication:

```
Router#config terminal
Enter configuration commands, one per line.  End with CNTL/Z.
Router(config)#line aux 0
Router(config)#login tacacs
Router(config)#exit
Router(config-line)#tacacs-server last-resort password
Router(config)#tacacs-server host 130.218.10.12
Router(config)#^Z
Router#
```

To set all line access to use TACACS, configure the other lines—console and VTYs 0 through 4—with the *login tacacs* command as well.

You can also tell the router to use TACACS for the enable or privileged-level password. To do so:

- Set the TACACS server with *tacacs-server host* if it is not already set.
- Configure TACACS enable authentication with *tacacs-server authenticate enable*.
- Configure the enable password to use TACACS with *enable use-tacacs*.
- Configure the enable password of last resort with *enable last-resort* so you can still access enable mode if the TACACS server is unavailable.

For example:

```
Router#config terminal
Enter configuration commands, one per line.  End with CNTL/Z.
Router(config)#tacacs-server host 130.218.10.5
Router(config)#tacacs-server authenticate enable
Router(config)#enable use-tacacs
Router(config)#enable last-resort password
Router(config)#^Z
Router#
```

configures the router to use TACACS for privilege access and to default to a locally configured enable password if the TACACS server is unavailable.

 Using regular TACACS for enable access allows anyone with a valid username and password to access privileged mode. Regular TACACS can't tell the different between a user-level authentication request and a privileged-level request. To solve this problem, use Extended TACACS or one of the AAA authentication methods such as RADIUS or TACACS+.

Disabling console, auxiliary, and VTY logins

If you do not need or cannot secure AUX or VTY access to the router, the safest measure is to disable logins on those ports completely. Disabling can be accomplished from global config mode by entering the AUX or VTY lines and disabling logins using the *login* and *no password* commands. The NSA's guide to router security also recommends that you use the *transport input none*, *no exec*, and *exec-timeout* commands for extra redundancy:

```
Router#config terminal
Enter configuration commands, one per line.  End with CNTL/Z.
Router(config)#line aux 0
Router(config-line)#login local
Router(config-line)#no password
Router(config-line)#transport input none
Router(config-line)#no exec
Router(config-line)#exec-timeout 0 1
Router(config-line)#^Z
Router#
```

This step is counterintuitive, but very important. Intuitively, it seems that the command *no password* would allow anyone to log in without a password. Likewise, intuitively, it seems that the command *no login* would disable logins completely. In reality, the opposite is true. Using the command *no login* on a line will allow anyone to log in without a password! The *no password* command removes the password but tells the router not to allow anyone to log in.

Disabling logins can be tricky. Under a line, the *no login* command overrides everything else. Look at the following configuration:

```
line vty 0 4
 password vty-password
 no login
```

A password is set, but the password is useless since the *no login* command allows anyone to log in without a password:

```
% telnet RouterOne
Trying RouterOne...
Connected to RouterOne.
Escape character is '^]'.

Router>
```

No password is required! In the following configuration, however:

```
line vty 0 4
 login
```

the *login* command is used and no password is set, but everyone is denied access:

```
% telnet RouterOne
Trying RouterOne...
Connected to RouterOne.
Escape character is '^]'.
```

```
Password required, but none set
Connection closed by foreign host.
```

TFTP Access

TFTP provides no methods of authentication; any TFTP client that knows the file-name can download the file. TFTP is normally used only when a router needs upgrading and represents a minimal security risk. However, routers are occasionally set to automatically download their configuration from a TFTP server at every reboot. This automatic download provides a security risk. If attackers are able to compromise the TFTP server and modify the configuration files that reside on that server, they can then attempt to crash the router, causing it to load the compromised configuration as it boots back up. If there are reasons why your routers must use TFTP servers for their configuration files, then the security of the router depends directly on the security of the TFTP server.

Additionally, newer routers can be configured to serve as TFTP servers with other TFTP clients downloading files from the router. If this feature is used, it should be turned on only for the duration of the transfer and then immediately turned off. Do not leave your routers configured as TFTP servers. Doing so invites an attacker to simply download your IOS versions and your configuration files.

Remote Administration

The console port is useful only if you have physical access to the router. This physical access is not always convenient. Many network administrators are responsible for national and international networks. These administrators require a way to monitor and administer a router from anywhere in the world. Cisco routers provide three main methods of remote administration. The first is an out-of-band method through dial-up on the AUX port; the other two are in-band VTY and HTTP access. These in-band methods can be used only when the network is functional.

Danger of Remote Administration

Some dangers are inherent to remote administration, and it is important to recognize what they are in order prevent them. Depending on how authentication and authorization are configured, common dangers include:

Spoofing
>If authentication depends on a trusted network or trusted IP address, attackers can create packets with fake source addresses, making the router believe that a packet came from a trusted source.

Trusted-host compromise

If authorization depends on a trusted host, attackers can compromise that host and make modifications to grant themselves access. A central access control server (ACS) such as TACACS or RADIUS would be a prime target for an attacker. If attackers could hack into the ACS, they could create an account to give themselves access to every router or system that relies on that ACS.

Sniffing

Sniffing used to be a difficult attack that required significant knowledge to perform, but current programs automatically capture and record logins and passwords as they are sent across the network. This makes sniffing a significant threat when logging into routers remotely.

Brute force attacks

If attackers can get a login prompt, then they can attempt to guess login names and passwords. A moderately skilled attacker can easily write a program that automates the guessing process. By default, routers do not limit unsuccessful login attempts, nor do they log them. Logging can be configured through AAA, however.

Hijacked sessions

Many TCP sessions are susceptible to hijacking. When this occurs, an attacker takes over a connection, such as a Telnet session, after you have logged in and authenticated yourself. If attackers can take over your connection, they then have the same access to the router as you do.

Table 3-1 lists common defenses to prevent these types of attacks when administering a router remotely.

Table 3-1. Preventing remote administration dangers

Danger	Prevention
Spoofing	Implement antispoofing filters (see Chapter 9), use encrypted sessions such as SSH, and use out-of-band management.
Trusted-host compromise	Make sure all trusted hosts are well hardened and constantly monitored for security.
Sniffing	Use encrypted protocols such as SSH, out-of-band management, or one-time passwords.
Brute force attacks	Choose strong passwords (see Chapter 4) and use filters to limit access to only a few IP addresses.
Hijacked sessions	Use encrypted protocols such as SSH and use out-of-band management. (Note: SSHv1 makes hijacked sessions harder, but still possible.)

Remote administration is extremely useful, but its security should be given a lot of thought.

Dial-up Access

The AUX port's primary purpose is to provide out-of-band remote administration capabilities through a modem. Once a modem is attached to the AUX port, it becomes a point of attack that grants access into your router and your entire network. Before attaching a modem to the AUX port, give the AUX port its own password. Do not rely only on the modem to provide secure access. This helps prevent several security problems, such as the modem being misconfigured or someone gaining physical access to the router, removing the modem, and using the unprotected AUX port to gain access. Besides AUX port password protection, several other steps can be taken to secure dial-up access. These steps include password protecting the modem itself, using callback features that require administrators to call from specific predefined numbers, and restricting the phone numbers that are allowed to call into your modems.

Password protecting the modem is specific to each modem, but callback security can be configured on the router itself. There are two types of callback access. First, remote users dial in, authenticate themselves, and ask the modem to call them back at their current number. The primary purpose of this method is to allow remote users to avoid hotel and long-distance charges. The other method is to have remote users dial in, authenticate themselves, and have the modem callback to a predetermined phone number. This means that access is restricted to a single phone line, so you lose some flexibility, but security is greatly enhanced.

If you want the security of single number callback with the flexibility of using out-of-band administration from anywhere, set up and secure an SSH server somewhere on another network, attach a modem to the server, and configure the router to use that number as the single callback number. Then you can SSH into the server from anywhere and from there dial into the router with callback security.

A word of warning, however: this works only if the SSH server is reachable, so it has to be located on another network that doesn't rely on the router you are trying to administer.

Callback access is linked to a specific username, so you should create separate accounts for each administrator who will need secure dial-up access. To establish callback security on a router, perform the following steps:

1. Enable EXEC-mode callback with the *service exec-callback* command.

2. Establish user accounts that specify a number to call back with the *username* command.

3. Configure a chat script to perform the callback using the *chat-script* command. Chat scripts define how the router talks with the modem and what it does at certain events such as disconnects or hang-ups.

4. Configure the auxiliary port to perform callback authentication. To do this:

    a. Configure it to use our chat scripts with the *script* command.

    b. Tell it to use local usernames for authentication with *login local*.

    c. Enable the modem for both inbound and outbound connections with *modem InOut*.

    d. Configure the modem to wait five seconds before dialing out using the *callback forced-wait* command. Doing so ensures that the modem has time to hang up the incoming connection before attempting to dial out.

    e. Configure flow control with the *flowcontrol* command.

Here is an example of configuring callback authentication on the AUX port:

```
Router#config terminal
Enter configuration commands, one per line.  End with CNTL/Z.
Router(config)#service exec-callback
Router(config)#username callme callback-dialstring "5554321357" password pass
Router(config)#chat-script offhook "" "ATH1" OK
Router(config)#chat-script rtp ABORT ERROR ABORT BUSY "" "AT" OK "ATDT \T" \
    TIMEOUT 45 CONNECT \c
Router(config)#line aux 0
Router(config-line)#script modem-off-hook offhook
Router(config-line)#script callback rtp
Router(config-line)#login local
Router(config-line)#modem InOut
Router(config-line)#callback forced-wait 5
Router(config-line)#flowcontrol hardware
Router(config-line)#^Z
Router#
```

 If you are using callback authentication, remember to configure your local modem to answer when the callback occurs. If you don't, the router will call back, but your modem won't answer. Setting autoanswer is usually done by sending a string similar to ats0=1 to the modem.

Another option to securing out-of-band modem-based access to your router is to have your telephone company set up a closed user group. Provide the telephone company with a list of numbers that are allowed to call the phone lines used by the modems on your router and for a monthly charge, they will limit access to only those numbers.

Reverse Telnet

Finally, there is a little-known feature of router ports that supports reverse Telnet, allowing access to physical ports through the network itself. This might be done to allow an administrator to telnet to a router and dial out through a modem connected to the AUX port.

Reverse Telnet access is granted if the transport input command is used under the line configuration. If enabled, the port will be accessible through the network on TCP port 20xx where xx is the TTY of the port on the router. To determine what network port is used, use the command *show line*. On a 2600, with a console port, an AUX port, and five VTYs, the output from this command looks like:

```
Router#show line
   Tty Typ    Tx/Rx    A Modem  Roty AccO AccI  Uses  Noise  Overruns  Int
*   0 CTY              - -       -   -    -      0     10     0/0       -
   65 AUX   9600/9600  - inout   -   -    -      6      0     0/0       -
   66 VTY              - -       -   -    -     51      0     0/0       -
   67 VTY              - -       -   -    -      0      0     0/0       -
   68 VTY              - -       -   -    -      0      0     0/0       -
   69 VTY              - -       -   -    -      0      0     0/0       -
   70 VTY              - -       -   -    -      0      0     0/0       -
```

The AUX TTY is number 65; therefore, the AUX port will listen to TCP port 2065 if reverse Telnet is enabled. For the sake of security, it is very important to disable network access to these ports. Disabling can be done with the *transport input* command by explicitly specifying *none*. To make sure that network access to the AUX port is disabled, you would specify:

```
Router#config terminal
Enter configuration commands, one per line.  End with CNTL/Z.
Router(config)#line aux 0
Router(config-line)#transport input none
Router(config-line)#^Z
Router#
```

This step disables reverse Telnet and secures the AUX port against access through the network. Make sure that all physical ports on your router use the *transport input none* command to disable network access.

VTY Access

VTY access is probably the most commonly used remote administration method. VTYs provide access to the router through the network itself, so the network must be functional before VTY access can be used. VTYs support multiple protocols, but the most commonly used one is Telnet. The problem with Telnet is that all information is passed over the network in clear text. A much more secure choice is the SSH protocol. With SSH, all information is encrypted, making sniffing much more difficult or useless. In addition to using SSH, VTY access should be limited by IP addresses. Only certain, predefined IP addresses should be allowed VTY access the router.

Disabling VTY access

In addition to disabling logins with the *login* and *no password* commands mentioned earlier, you can disable all access to the VTY ports by using the *transport input none* command.

You can also use the *no exec* and *exec-timeout* commands for redundant security:

```
Router#config terminal
Enter configuration commands, one per line.  End with CNTL/Z.
Router(config)#line vty 0 4
Router(config-line)#transport input none
Router(config-line)#exec-timeout 0 1
Router(config-line)#no exec
Router(config-line)#^Z
Router#
```

Using these commands completely disables the ability to connect to all VTY ports with any protocol. With the *login/no password* method, the Telnet port remains open, but users receive the message *Password required, but none set*. Using *transport input none* closes the port so that no one can even make a connection:

```
% telnet RouterOne
Trying RouterOne...
telnet: Unable to connect to remote host: Connection refused
```

SSH

With Telnet, it is just a matter of time until someone sniffs your passwords and compromises your routers. Many Cisco routers currently support SSH, but only if they are running IOS images that support IPSec. Currently, Cisco supports only SSH Version 1. SSHv1 is still susceptible to session hijacking, though less so than clear text protocols such as Telnet. To enable SSH you need to:

- Configure a hostname for your router with the *hostname* command.
- Configure a domain for your router with the *ip domain-name* command.
- Generate RSA encryption keys by using the *crypto key generate rsa* command. This command will prompt you for a modulus size. Cisco recommends a minimum size of 1024. A size of 2048 will increase your security, but may decrease your performance.
- Enable SSH access with the *ip ssh* command (indicating the timeout value and number of retries).
- Configure each line to use SSH using the *transport input* command.

For example:

```
Router#config terminal
Enter configuration commands, one per line.  End with CNTL/Z.
Router(config)#hostname RouterOne
RouterOne(config)#ip domain-name mydomain.com
RouterOne(config)#crypto key generate rsa
The name for the keys will be: RouterOne
Choose the size of the key modulus in the range of 360 to 2048 for your
  General Purpose Keys. Choosing a key modulus greater than 512 may take
  a few minutes.
```

```
How many bits in the modulus [512]: 1024
Generating RSA keys ...
[OK]
RouterOne(config)#ip ssh time-out 60
RouterOne(config)#ip ssh authentication-retries 2
RouterOne(config)#line vty 0 4
RouterOne(config-line)#transport input ssh
RouterOne(config-line)#^Z
RouterOne#
```

enables SSH on *RouterOne* and sets all five VTYs to allow SSH access only.

If you have a router or IOS image that does not support SSH, don't use Telnet! Instead, set up a secure SSH server on your internal network. The server should be located in a secure location and be on a trusted network. Then, from anywhere on the Internet, you can SSH to the server and telnet from it to the router. This way, the connection into your network is encrypted, and only the last part of the connection—between the SSH server and the router—is unencrypted. This method still leaves you vulnerable to insider attackers (i.e., those who can monitor the connection between the SSH server and the router), but it keeps the rest of the world from sniffing your password or hijacking your connection.

 SSH access cannot use line authentication; you have to either configure local usernames and passwords with the *username* command or use AAA authentication.

Limiting VTY access by IP

By default, VTY ports allow any IP address to attempt authentication. This allows an attacker to try brute force password guessing against your routers from anywhere on the Internet. If VTYs are not disabled, they need to be restricted so that only a few select IPs are allowed to even attempt to log in. This can be done using access control lists (ACLs) and the access-class command under the VTY lines.

To limit VTY access, you:

1. Create an ACL.

2. Apply the ACL to all VTY lines with the *access-class* command.

For example, limiting VTY access to only the IPs 130.218.10.12 and 130.218.20.5 would look like:

```
Router#config terminal
Enter configuration commands, one per line.  End with CNTL/Z.
Router(config)#access-list 10 permit 130.218.10.12
Router(config)#access-list 10 permit 130.218.20.5
Router(config)#access-list 10 deny any
Router(config)#line vty 0 4
Router(config-line)#access-class 10 in
Router(config-line)#^Z
Router#
```

With the preceding configuration, only the two specified IPs are allowed to connect to the VTY ports and attempt authentication.

Additional VTY settings

In addition to using SSH and limiting access to a few select IPs, a couple of additional measures can help make VTY access more secure. The first measure is the *exec-timeout* command. This command tells the router how long to wait before disconnecting an idle session. The default timeout for idle sessions is ten minutes. It is recommended that you change this timeout to five minutes or less. The *exec-timeout* command takes two arguments—first minutes and then seconds.

Additionally, you can use the *service tcp-keepalives-in* command to make sure that your VTYs don't fill up with orphaned connections. If the remote client crashes or is disconnected abnormally, the VTY will still believe that the remote client is attached. This can cause error messages similar to *Connection refused by remote host*. Using *service tcp-keepalives-in*, the router can watch all incoming connections, determine whether the remote end disconnects abnormally, and reset the connection, freeing up the VTY port.

Setting *tcp-keepalives* is done globally, and setting the *exec-timeout* is done under each line:

```
Router#config terminal
Enter configuration commands, one per line.  End with CNTL/Z.
Router(config)#service tcp-keepalives-in
Router(config)#line vty 0 4
Router(config-line)#exec-timeout 5 0
Router(config-line)#^Z
Router#
```

HTTP/Web Access

Cisco has added HTTP access to allow monitoring and management of the router through a web browser. This feature, however, has several security problems. First, all passwords through HTTP are sent across the network in clear text with no encryption. Second, all content is sent across the Net in clear text. Finally, the HTTP protocol provides no way to use token-based or one-time passwords. Therefore, I highly recommend that HTTP access to the router be completely disabled with the *no ip http server* command:

```
Router#config terminal
Enter configuration commands, one per line.  End with CNTL/Z.
Router(config)#no ip http server
Router(config)#^Z
Router#
```

If HTTP access must be enabled, it must be set up as securely as possible. Setting it up securely involves restricting access with the *ip http access-class* command and choosing a secure authentication method with the *ip http authentication* command.

Limiting HTTP access by IP

Limiting HTTP access by IP is similar to limiting VTY access. You create an appropriate ACL and apply it with the *ip http access-class* command.

Limiting HTTP access to the IP 130.218.40.15 would look like:

```
Router#config terminal
Enter configuration commands, one per line.  End with CNTL/Z.
Router(config)#access-list 20 permit 130.218.40.15
Router(config)#access-list 20 deny any
Router(config)#ip http access-class 20
Router(config)#^Z
Router#
```

If the IPs that need HTTP access are the same as those that need VTY access, then you can even use the same ACL that was created to limit VTY access.

HTTP authentication

By default, HTTP uses the enable password and defaults to privileged-level access. HTTP router access can also be set up to use local, TACACS, and AAA authentication methods. It supports all 16 authorization levels. These levels are explained in Chapter 4, but each level can be accessed with a URL similar to *http://MyRouter/level/X*, where X is the authorization level you want to access. Only users who are authorized for a specific privilege level are allowed log in. You can access the two default levels—user and privilege—through both *http://MyRouter* or *http://MyRouter/level/15* for privileged level and *http://MyRouter/level/01* for user level.

To change the way HTTP authenticates on the router, once you have your local usernames, TACACS server, or AAA authentication method set up, you can use the command *ip http authentication*:

```
Router#config terminal
Enter configuration commands, one per line.  End with CNTL/Z.
Router(config)#ip http authentication type
Router(config)#^Z
Router#
```

In this example, **type** is replaced with **enable**, **local**, **tacacs**, or **aaa**. Because of the inherent weakness in HTTP authentication, it is important to change the authentication method from the default of using the enable password to a different method.

Protection with IPSec

While a router that allows only console or SSH access is ideal, you may sometimes be required to set up configurations that you know have security vulnerabilities. Your organization might require SNMP Version 1 or need to allow certain administrators Telnet access to the router. A way to help mitigate the risk associated with these protocols and to add an additional layer of security to your existing methods is to use IPSec. IPSec is traditionally used to set up VPNs between networks or between a roaming user and her home network. If your routers and management stations all support IPSec, you can create a VPN between the router and management stations, encrypting all traffic sent between the two.

A full tutorial on IPSec and VPNs is out of the scope of this book, but a brief overview on how to configure your router for an IPSec VPN to the management station follows. In this example, the router is named *RouterOne*, and the management station has an IP of 130.18.10.10. Also, this example uses preshared keys (a password manually configured on both sides). Advanced VPN solutions can use key management systems instead of statically configured keys.

To configure the router end of your VPN, you must:

1. Set up ISAKMP with the preshared key. ISAKMP defines how the key exchange is implemented.

2. Create an Extended ACL on the router. With IPSec, Extended ACLs are used to configure which packets are encrypted and which aren't. This configuration lets an interface support both encrypted and regular traffic. In relation to IPSec, *permit* means encrypt and *deny* means do not encrypt.

3. Create IPSec transforms. Transforms are Cisco's way of defining what type of authentication and encryption is used for each IPSec packet. This example uses some standard transforms, but may need to be changed depending on which ones the management station supports.

4. Create a crypto map. The crypto map ties our ISAKMP, ACL, and transform configurations together. The crypto map is also configured with the IP address of the management station with which we create a VPN.

5. Apply the crypto map to the router interface. After creating the crypto map, it must be applied to the appropriate interface to take effect.

Setting up ISAKMP

To set up ISAKMP with a preshared key, you must:

1. Use the *crypto isakmp policy* command to create a policy. Policies are differentiated by numbers. This example will use number 10.

2. Use the *authentication pre-share* command to define the preshared password we are using for the VPN.

Following is an example of configuring ISAKMP on the router:

```
RouterOne#config terminal
Enter configuration commands, one per line.  End with CNTL/Z.
RouterOne(config)#crypto isakmp policy 10
RouterOne(config-isakmp)#authentication pre-share
RouterOne(config-isakmp)#^Z
```

Creating the IPSec Extended ACL

When applied to an IPSec crypto map, the ACL defines which packets are encrypted and which are normal traffic. In this example, the management station is 130.18.10. 10, so the ACL will encrypt (permit) traffic to this IP and not encrypt (deny) traffic to all other IPs:

```
RouterOne#config terminal
Enter configuration commands, one per line.  End with CNTL/Z.
RouterOne(config)#access-list 150 permit ip host 130.18.10.10 host RouterOne
RouterOne(config)#access-list 150 deny ip any any
RouterOne(config)#^Z
```

If you have more than one management station with which you are creating IPSec connections, you would also enter them in the preceding ACL.

Creating IPSec Transforms

Transforms define what types of authentication and encryption are supported by this VPN. The following transforms are fairly standard—HMAC-MD5 for authentication and DES for encryption—but they may need to be modified depending on what authentication and encryption the management station supports. Transforms are defined using the *crypto ipsec transform-set* command. In this example, the transform is named *TransOne*:

```
RouterOne#config terminal
Enter configuration commands, one per line.  End with CNTL/Z.
RouterOne(config)#crypto ipsec transform-set TransOne ah-md5-hmac esp-des
RouterOne(cfg-crypto-trans)#^Z
```

Creating the Crypto Map

The crypto map takes the three preceding configuration options and ties them into a single entity that can be applied to the interface. Defining a crypto map requires that you:

1. Create the map with the *crypto map* command. This command requires the ISAKMP policy that was defined in the first step. In this example, the policy was identified as number 10.

2. Define the IP of the management station with which we are creating an IPSec VPN. This is done with the *set peer* command.

3. Define the transform set to use for this VPN. This is done with the *set transform-set* command.

4. Finally, identify the ACL defining which packets are encrypted and which packets are normal with the *match address* command. The ACL in this example is 150, so that the number is used with the command.

The following example defines the example crypto map and names it *MyMapOne*:

```
RouterOne#config terminal
Enter configuration commands, one per line.  End with CNTL/Z.
RouterOne(config)#crypto map MyMapOne 10 ipsec-isakmp
RouterOne(config-crypto-map)#set peer 130.18.10.10
RouterOne(config-crypto-map)#set transform-set TransOne
RouterOne(config-crypto-map)#match address 150
RouterOne(config-crypto-map)#^Z
```

Applying the Crypto Map to an Interface

Finally, you must apply the crypto map to the interface on which you want the VPN to be established. The following example uses interface Serial 0/1 as the interface with which the management station will VPN:

```
RouterOne#config terminal
Enter configuration commands, one per line.  End with CNTL/Z.
RouterOne(config)#int Serial 0/1
RouterOne(config-if)#crypto map MyMapOne
RouterOne(config-if)#^Z
```

Now all you need to do is configure your management station to peer with the IP address of the interface, and all traffic between the management station and the router will be encrypted.

Basic Access Control Security Checklist

- Secure physical access to the router. (See Appendix B).
- Secure console access with the *login* and *password* commands.
- Disable or secure AUX access with the *login* and *password* commands.
- Disable or secure all VTY access with the *login* and *password* commands.
- Do not use the *no login* command under any line (*con/aux/vty*) configurations.
- Set the enable password using the *enable secret* command.
- In organizations in which multiple administrators access a router, enable accountability by requiring administrators to have separate accounts to access the router. This can be accomplished through local usernames or more centralized methods involving network access servers.
- Do not use TACACS and Extended TACACS in favor of TACACS+, RADIUS, or Kerberos.

- If any version of TACACS is used for user-level authentications, set the method of last resort to the privileged password (set with *enable secret*) and not to default to open access with no authentication.
- Do not use standard TACACS for privileged-level access.
- If any version of TACACS is used for the enable password—privileged-level access—then set the method of last resort to the enable secret password and not to automatically succeed.
- Make sure the router does not use TFTP to automatically load its configuration at every reboot. If it must, then harden and secure the TFTP server.
- Do not configure the router to serve as a TFTP server.
- With dial-up access to the router, make sure both the AUX port and the modem are password protected.
- With dial-up access to the router, configure callback security to a predefined number, or make sure the telephone company uses a closed user group to restrict which numbers are allowed to call your modems.
- Never connect a modem to the console port.
- Disable reverse Telnet to all physical ports.
- Disable Telnet in favor of SSH on all VTY lines.
- If insecure protocols such at Telnet or HTTP must be used, use IPSec to encrypt all vulnerable traffic.
- Make sure all VTY access uses ACLs to restrict access to a few secured IPs.
- Set the *exec-timeout* on all VTYs to five minutes or less.
- Enable the global command *service tcp-keepalives-in*.
- Disable HTTP access to the router.
- If HTTP access must be used:
    — Limit its use to secure networks.
    — Only use it over IPSec.
    — Restrict access with ACLs to a few secured IPs.
    — Change the HTTP authentication method from the default enable password.

CHAPTER 4

Passwords and Privilege Levels

Passwords are the core of Cisco routers' access control methods. Chapter 3 addressed basic access control and using passwords locally and from access control servers. This chapter talks about how Cisco routers store passwords, how important it is that the passwords chosen are strong passwords, and how to make sure that your routers use the most secure methods for storing and handling passwords. It then discusses privilege levels and how to implement them.

Password Encryption

Cisco routers have three methods of representing passwords in the configuration file. From weakest to strongest, they include clear text, Vigenere encryption, and MD5 hash algorithm. Clear-text passwords are represented in human-readable format. Both the Vigenere and MD5 encryption methods obscure passwords, but each has its own strengths and weaknesses.

Vigenere Versus MD5

The main difference between Vigenere and MD5 is that Vigenere is reversible, while MD5 is not. Being reversible makes it easier for an attacker to break the encryption and obtain the passwords. Being unreversible means that an attacker must use much slower brute force guessing attacks in an attempt to obtain the passwords.

Ideally, all router passwords would use strong MD5 encryption, but the way certain protocols, such as CHAP and PAP, work, routers must be able to decode the original password to perform authentication. This need to decode specific passwords means that Cisco routers will continue to use reversible encryption for some passwords—at least until such authentication protocols are rewritten or replaced.

Clear-Text Passwords

Chapter 3 sets passwords using line passwords, local username passwords, and the *enable secret* command. A *show run* provides the following:

```
enable secret 5 $1$Guks$Ct2/uAcSKHkcxNKyavE1i1
enable password enable-password
!
username jdoe password 0 jdoe-password
username rsmith password 0 rsmith-password
!
line con 0
 exec-timeout 5 0
 password console-password
 login local
 transport input none
line aux 0
 exec-timeout 5 0
 password aux-password
 login tacacs
 transport input none
line vty 0 4
 exec-timeout 5 0
 password vty-password
 login
 transport input ssh
```

The highlighted parts of the configuration are the passwords. Notice that all passwords, except the *enable secret* password, are in clear text. This clear text poses a significant security risk. Anyone who can view a copy of the configuration file—whether through shoulder surfing or off a backup server—can see the router passwords. We need a way to make sure that all passwords in the router configuration file are encrypted.

service password-encryption

The first method of encryption that Cisco provides is through the command *service password-encryption*. This command obscures all clear-text passwords in the configuration using a Vigenere cipher. You enable this feature from global configuration mode.

```
Router#config terminal
Enter configuration commands, one per line.  End with CNTL/Z.
Router(config)#service password-encryption
Router(config)#^Z
```

Now a *show run* command no longer displays the password in humanly readable format.

```
enable secret 5 $1$Guks$Ct2/uAcSKHkcxNKyavE1i1
enable password 7 02030A5A46160E325F59060B01
```

```
 !
 username jdoe password 7 09464A061C480713181F13253920
 username rsmith password 7 095E5D0410111F5F1B0D17393C2B3A37
 !
 line con 0
  exec-timeout 5 0
  password 7 110A160B041D0709493A2A373B243A3017
  login local
  transport input none
 line aux 0
  exec-timeout 5 0
  password 7 0005061E494B0A151C36435C0D
  login tacacs
  transport input all
 line vty 0 4
  exec-timeout 5 0
  password 7 095A5A1054151601181B0B382F
  login
  transport input ssh
```

The only password not affected by the *service password-encryption* command is the *enable secret* password. It always uses the MD5 encryption scheme.

While the *service password-encryption* command is beneficial and should be enabled on all routers, remember that the command uses an easily reversible cipher. Some commercial programs and freely available Perl scripts instantly decode any passwords encrypted with this cipher. This means that the *service password-encryption* command protects only against casual viewers—someone looking over your shoulder—and not against someone who obtains a copy of the configuration file and runs a decoder against the encrypted passwords. Finally, *service password-encryption* does not protect all secret values such as SNMP community strings and RADIUS or TACACS keys.

Enable Security

The enable, or privileged, password has an additional level of encryption that should always be used. The privileged-level password should always use the MD5 encryption scheme.

In early IOS configurations, the privileged password was set with the *enable password* command and was represented in the configuration file in clear text:

```
enable password ena-password
```

For additional security, Cisco added the *service password-encryption* command to obscure all clear-text passwords:

```
service password-encryption
enable password 7 02030A5A46160E325F59060B01
```

However, as explained earlier, this uses the weak Vigenere cipher. Because of the importance of the privileged-level password and the fact that it doesn't need to be reversible, Cisco added the *enable secret* command that uses strong MD5 encryption:

```
Router#config terminal
Enter configuration commands, one per line.  End with CNTL/Z.
Router(config)#enable secret my-secret-password
Router(config)#^Z
```

A *show run* now displays:

```
enable secret 5 $1$Guks$Ct2/uAcSKHkcxNKyavE1i1e
```

This type of encryption cannot be reversed. The only way to attack it is though brute force methods.

You should always use the *enable secret* command instead of *enable password*. The *enable password* command is provided only for backward compatibility. If both are set, for example:

```
enable password 7 02030A5A46160E325F59060B01
enable secret 5 $1$Guks$Ct2/uAcSKHkcxNKyavE1i1e
```

the *enable secret* password takes precedence and the *enable password* command is ignored.

 Many organizations begin using the insecure *enable password* command, and then migrate to using the *enable secret* command. Often, however, they use the same passwords for both the *enable password* and *enable secret* commands. Using the same passwords defeats the purpose of the stronger encryption provided by the *enable secret* command. Attackers can simply decode the weak encryption from the *enable password* command to get the router's password. To avoid this weakness, be sure to use different passwords for each command—or better yet, don't use the enable password command at all.

Strong Passwords

In addition to using encryption to keep passwords from appearing in human-readable form, secure password protection requires the use of strong passwords. There are two requirements for strong passwords. First, they are difficult to guess or crack. Second, they are easy to remember. If the password is based on a word found in a dictionary—a name, a place, and so on—the password is weak. If the password is a complete random string of letters and numbers, the password is strong, but users end up writing the password down because they can't remember it. To demonstrate how easy it is to crack weak passwords, the following passwords were encrypted with the strong MD5 encryption:

- *hello*
- *Enter0*

- *9spot*
- *8twelve8*
- *ilcic4l*

A brute force password-cracking program was used to see how long it would take to guess each password.

On a Sun Ultra 5 with 512MB of RAM and a 333MHz processor, the first password, *hello*, took less than five seconds to crack. This is the same amount of time it would take to guess most words in the English language (or a word in any other language, if the attacker included foreign language dictionaries). After four hours, the password cracker has guessed the next three passwords as well. Any password based on a word—English or foreign—is vulnerable to brute force attacks.

The last password looks random and was still not cracked when the password cracker stopped running three days later. The problem is remembering a password like this one. See the upcoming sidebar, "Choosing and Remembering Strong Passwords" for tips on choosing an appropriate password.

Keeping Configuration Files Secure

Except for the *enable secret* password, all passwords stored on Cisco routers are weakly encrypted. If someone were to get a copy of a router configuration file, it would take only a few seconds to run it through a program to decode all weakly encrypted passwords. The first protection is to keep the configuration files secured.

You should always have a backup of each router's configuration file. You should probably have multiple backups. However, each of these backups must be kept in a secure location. This means that they are not stored on a public server or on each network administrator's desktop. Additionally, backups of all routers are usually kept on the same system. If this system is insecure, and an attacker can gain access, he has hit the jackpot—the complete configuration of your entire network, all access list setups, weak passwords, SNMP community strings, and so on. To avoid this problem, wherever backup configuration files are kept, it is best to keep them encrypted. That way, even if an attacker gains access to the backup files, they are useless.

Encryption on an insecure system, however, provides a false sense of security. If attackers can break into the insecure system, they can set up a key logger and capture everything that is typed on that system. This includes the passwords to decrypt the configuration files. In this case, an attacker just has to wait until the administrator types in the password, and your encryption is compromised.

Another option is to make sure your backup configuration files don't contain any passwords. This requires that you remove the password from your backup configurations manually or create scripts that strip out this information automatically.

Choosing and Remembering Strong Passwords

The best way to create a password that is easy to remember but difficult to crack is to use pass phrases. Cisco routers support passwords of up to 25 characters. So create a sentence and use that instead of just a password. When you can't use a sentence, choose memorable, but strong, six- to eight-character passwords.

When testing the sample passwords *hello*, *Enter0*, *9spot*, *8twelve8*, and *ilcic4l,* the only password that wasn't cracked was *ilcic4l*. The problem is how to remember a password like this. The secret is that this password looks random, but it is not. To create this password, an easily remembered sentence was created. In this case, the sentence was, "I like chocolate ice cream for lunch." Then the first letter of each word was used to create the base of the password: *ilcicfl*. Next, the number 4 was put in place of the word *for*. This provides *ilcic4l*—a password that is easy to remember, but difficult to crack.

This technique can be modified in any way you like. Take the second letter of each word instead of the first. Change every *e* to a *3*, every *a* to an *@*, or every *t* to a +. Add numbers to the beginning or the end of the password—whatever you can think of.

Finally, another key to creating strong passwords is using a different password on each system. That way, if someone guesses or steals one of your password, they can't use that password to access every system you have an account on. Now there is a problem of remembering a different password for every system you access. There is a solution to this as well. You can modify the preceding technique to help you remember different passwords for every system. For example, take the password used previously, *ilcic4l*, and modify it for each system that you access. First come up with a formula. A simple one would be to take the first letter of the system name you are connecting to and replace the first letter of the password with that letter. Then do the same for the last letter. If connecting to a system called *Router1*, the password for that system would be *Rlcic41*. If connecting to *Firewall-One*, the password is *Flcic4e*. These simple examples produce numerous strong passwords that are easy to remember but difficult to crack. You can get as creative as you want in coming up with sentences and formulas. In fact, the more creative you get, the stronger your passwords will be.

 Administrators should be very careful not to access routers from insecure or untrusted systems. Encryption or SSH does no good if an attacker has compromised the system you're working on and can use a key logger to record everything you type.

Finally, avoid storing your configuration files on your TFTP server. TFTP provides no authentication, so you should move files out of the TFTP download directory as quickly as possible to limit your exposure.

Privilege Levels

By default, Cisco routers have three levels of privilege—zero, user, and privileged. Zero-level access allows only five commands—logout, enable, disable, help, and exit. User level (level 1) provides very limited read-only access to the router, and privileged level (level 15) provides complete control over the router. This all-or-nothing setting can work in small networks with one or two routers and one administrator, but larger networks require additional flexibility. To provide this flexibility, Cisco routers can be configured to use 16 different privilege levels from 0 to 15.

Changing Privilege Levels

Displaying your current privilege level is done with the *show privilege* command, and changing privilege levels can be done using the *enable* and *disable* commands. Without any arguments, *enable* will attempt to change to level 15 and *disable* will change to level 1. Both commands take a single argument that specifies the level you want to change to. The *enable* command is used to gain more access by moving up levels:

```
Router>show privilege
Current privilege level is 1
Router>enable 5
Password: level-5-password
Router#show privilege
Current privilege level is 5
Router#
```

The *disable* command is used to give up access by moving down levels:

```
Router#show privilege
Current privilege level is 5
Router#disable 2
Router#show privilege
Current privilege level is 2
Router#
```

Notice that a password is required to gain more access; no password is required when lowering your level of access. The router requires reauthentication every time you attempt to gain more privileges, but nothing is needed to give up privileges.

Default Privilege Levels

The bottom and least privileged level is level 0. This is the only other level besides 1 and 15 that is configured by default on Cisco routers. This level has only five commands that allow you to log out or attempt to enter a higher level:

```
Router#disable 0
Router>?
Exec commands:
  disable  Turn off privileged commands
  enable   Turn on privileged commands
```

```
    exit    Exit from the EXEC
    help    Description of the interactive help system
    logout  Exit from the EXEC
Router>
```

Next is level 1, the default user level. This level provides the user with many more commands that allow the user to display router information, telnet to other systems, and test network connectivity with *ping* and *traceroute*. Level 2, which is not enabled by default, adds a few additional *show* and *clear* commands, but provides no opportunity for a user to reconfigure the router. Finally, level 15 allows full access to all router commands.

Privilege-Level Passwords

To use the *enable* command to access a privilege level, a password must be set for that level. If you try to enter a level with no password, you get the error message *No password set*. Setting privilege-level passwords can be done with the *enable secret level* command. The following example enables and sets a password for privilege level 5:

```
Router#config terminal
Enter configuration commands, one per line.  End with CNTL/Z.
Router(config)#enable secret level 5 level5-password
Router(config)#^Z
Router#
```

Now we can enter level 5 with the *enable 5* command.

 Just as default passwords can be set with either the *enable secret* or the *enable password* command, passwords for other privilege levels can be set with the *enable password level* or *enable secret level* commands. However, the *enable password level* command is provided for backward compatibility and should not be used.

Line Privilege Levels

Lines (CON, AUX, VTY) default to level 1 privileges. This can be changed using the *privilege level* command under each line. To change the default privilege level of the AUX port, you would type the following:

```
Router#config terminal
Enter configuration commands, one per line.  End with CNTL/Z.
Router(config)#line aux 0
Router(config-line)#privilege level 4
Router(config-line)#^Z
Router#
```

Or, to change the default privilege level of all VTY access to level 12:

```
Router#config terminal
Enter configuration commands, one per line.  End with CNTL/Z.
Router(config)#line vty 0 4
```

```
Router(config-line)#privilege level 12
Router(config-line)#^Z
Router#
```

Username Privilege Levels

Finally, a username can have a privilege level associated with it. This is useful when you want specific users to default to higher privileges. The *username privilege* command is used to set the privilege level for a user:

```
Router#config terminal
Enter configuration commands, one per line.  End with CNTL/Z.
Router(config)#username jdoe privilege 5
Router(config)#username rsmith privilege 12
Router(config)#^Z
Router#
```

Changing Command Privilege Levels

By default, all router commands fall under levels 1 or 15. Creating additional privilege levels isn't very useful unless the default privilege level of some router commands is also changed. Once the default privilege level of a command is changed, only those who have that level access or above are allowed to run that command. These changes are made with the *privilege* command. The following example changes the default level of the *telnet* command to level 2:

```
Router#config terminal
Enter configuration commands, one per line.  End with CNTL/Z.
Router(config)#privilege exec level 2 telnet
Router(config)#^Z
Router#
```

Now no one with user-level (level 1) access can run the *telnet* command. Level 2 access is required.

Privilege Mode Example

Here is an example of how an organization might use privilege levels to access the router without giving everyone the level 15 password.

Assume that the organization has a few highly paid network administrators, a few junior network administrators, and a computer operations center for troubleshooting problems. This organization wants the highly paid network administrators to be the only ones with complete (level 15) access to the routers, but also wants the junior administrators have more limited access to the router that will allow them to help with debugging and troubleshooting. Finally, the computer operations center needs to be able to run the *clear line* command so they can reset the modem dial-up connection for the administrators if needed; however, they shouldn't be able to telnet from the router to other systems.

The highly paid administrators will have complete level 15 access. A level 10 will be created for the junior administrators to give them access to the *debug* and *telnet* commands. Finally, a level 2 will be created for the operations center to give them access to the *clear line* command, but not the *telnet* command:

```
Router#config terminal
Enter configuration commands, one per line.  End with CNTL/Z.
Router(config)#username admin-joe privilege 15 password joes-password
Router(config)#username admin-carl privilege 15 password carls-password
Router(config)#username junior-jeff privilege 10 password jeffs-password
Router(config)#username junior-jay privilege 10 password jays-password
Router(config)#username ops-fred privilege 2 password freds-password
Router(config)#username ops-pat privilege 2 password pats-password
Router(config)#privilege exec level 10 telnet
Router(config)#privilege exec level 10 debug
Router(config)#privilege exec level 2 clear line
Router(config)#^Z
Router#
```

Recommended Privilege-Level Changes

The NSA guide to Cisco router security recommends that the following commands be moved from their default privilege level 1 to privilege level 15—*connect*, *telnet*, *rlogin*, *show ip access-lists*, *show access-lists*, and *show logging*. Changing these levels limits the usefulness of the router to an attacker who compromises a user-level account.

To change the privilege level of these commands, you would:

```
RouterOne#config terminal
Enter configuration commands, one per line.  End with CNTL/Z.
RouterOne(config)#privilege exec level 15 connect
RouterOne(config)#privilege exec level 15 telnet
RouterOne(config)#privilege exec level 15 rlogin
RouterOne(config)#privilege exec level 15 show ip access-lists
RouterOne(config)#privilege exec level 15 show access-lists
RouterOne(config)#privilege exec level 15 show logging
RouterOne(config)#privilege exec level 1 show ip
RouterOne(config)#^Z
```

The final *privilege exec level 1 show ip* returns the *show* and *show ip* commands to level 1, enabling all other default level 1 commands to still function.

Password Checklist

This checklist summarizes the important security information presented in this chapter. A complete security checklist is provided in Appendix A.

- Enable *service password-encryption* on all routers.
- Set the privileged-level (level 15) password with the *enable secret* command and not with the *enable password* command.

- Make sure all passwords are strong passwords that are not based on English or foreign words.
- Make sure each router has different enable and user passwords.
- Keep backup configuration files encrypted on a secure server.
- Access routers only from secure or trusted systems.
- In large organizations with numerous personnel with router access, use additional privilege levels to restrict access to unnecessary commands.
- Reconfigure the *connect*, *telnet*, *rlogin*, *show ip access-lists*, *show access-lists*, and *show logging* commands to privilege level 15.

CHAPTER 5

AAA Access Control

AAA stands for authentication, authorization, accounting. This chapter will cover the authentication and authorization aspects of AAA, leaving the accounting details for Chapter 11. AAA access control provides much greater scalability and functionality than the basic access control methods discussed in Chapter 3. AAA can use local router configuration, TACACS+, RADIUS, and Kerberos for authentication and can utilize a TACACS+ or RADIUS for authorization.

TACACS+ and RADIUS can be used both for authentication and authorization, while Kerberos can be used only for authentication. Cisco-only networks usually choose TACACS+ because of its enhanced features. TACACS+, however, is proprietary to Cisco. Networks using equipment from multiple vendors usually choose RADIUS for its interoperability. Finally, organizations with existing Kerberos access servers can configure their routers to use those servers to control access to Cisco routers.

Enabling AAA

To use any of these authentication and authorization methods, you must first enable AAA on the router. The general steps for enabling AAA are:

1. Turn on AAA with the *aaa new-model* command.
2. Configure security protocol information if using an access control server (ACS).
3. Define methods that specify the type and order of authentication with the *aaa authentication* command.
4. Apply the authentication methods to each line and/or enable access.
5. Configure AAA authorization, if needed, with the *aaa authorization* command.

Local Authentication

Assume that the router configuration has the following users:

```
username jdoe password 7 09464A061C480713181F13253920
username rsmith password 7 095E5D0410111F5F1B0D17393C2B3A37
```

To take advantage of the AAA accounting features, you can enable AAA but use these locally defined usernames for access. To do so:

1. Enable AAA with *aaa new-model*.

2. Make the default AAA authentication method local using the *aaa authentication* command.

3. Apply the default AAA authentication method to each line:

```
Router#config terminal
Enter configuration commands, one per line.  End with CNTL/Z.
Router(config)#aaa new-model
Router(config)#aaa authentication login default local
Router(config)#line vty 0 4
Router(config-line)#login authentication default
Router(config-line)#exit
Router(config)#line aux 0
Router(config-line)#login authentication default
Router(config-line)#exit
Router(config)#line con 0
Router(config-line)#login authentication default
Router(config-line)#^Z
Router#
```

While AAA and local authentication provide greater accountability than non-AAA methods, local AAA authentication is not scalable, and all local passwords are stored in the configuration file using the weak Vigenere ciphers.

TACACS+ Authentication

TACACS+ is Cisco's proprietary and recommended access control protocol. TACACS+ has the benefits of running over TCP, encrypting the entire contents of packets between the ACS and the router, supporting multiple protocols, and providing authentication and authorization support. TACACS+, however, is proprietary, and if your ACS server needs to serve non-Cisco equipment, you may have difficulty. If you are going to implement an ACS server for your Cisco routers only, TACACS+ is definitely the choice to make. Configuring TACACS+ on a router is fairly straightforward, but since the packets are encrypted, both the router and the server must be preconfigured with an encryption key.

To configure a router to use a TACACS+ server, assuming that the server is configured with the key *MyTACACSkey*, you must:

1. Enable AAA with the *aaa new-model* command.

2. Tell the router what TACACS+ server to use with the *tacacs-server host* command.

3. Tell the router what the TACACS+ server key is with the *tacacs-server key* command.

4. Define the default AAA authentication method to be TACACS+ with the locally configured users as a backup in case the TACACS+ server isn't available.

5. Configure each line to use the default AAA authentication method.

Here is example of setting the AUX and VTY ports to use the TACACS+ server 130. 218.12.10:

```
Router#config terminal
Enter configuration commands, one per line.  End with CNTL/Z.
Router(config)#aaa new-model
Router(config)#tacacs-server host 130.218.12.10
Router(config)#tacacs-server key MyTACACSkey
Router(config)#aaa authentication login default group tacacs+ local
Router(config)#line aux 0
Router(config-line)#login authentication default
Router(config-line)#exit
Router(config)#line vty 0 4
Router(config-line)#login authentication default
Router(config-line)#^Z
Router#
```

 IOS Versions 12.0.5(T) and later use the *aaa authentication login default group tacacs+ enable* command. Earlier versions leave out the keyword *group* and use the *aaa authentication login default tacacs+ enable* command.

The router is now set up to use the TACACS+ server 130.218.12.10 for authentication. There is an important item to note when using the *aaa authentication login* command. The command tells the router to attempt to authenticate a user through TACACS+ first, and to use the locally configured enable password only if it fails to reach the server. If the TACACS+ server is unreachable for some reason, the router use the local enable password. If the TACACS+ server is reachable, but rejects users because they didn't authenticate themselves correctly, the router does not default to the enable password, but denies the users access.

TACACS+ Enable Password

You can also use TACACS+ for the enable password. If TACACS+ is already configured on your router, this can be done with the command:

aaa authentication enable default group tacacs+ enable

Otherwise, you need to:

1. Enable AAA, if not already enabled, with the *aaa new-model* command.

2. Tell the router what TACACS+ server to use with the *tacacs-server host* command.

3. Tell the router what the TACACS+ server key is.

4. Configure the enable password to use the TACACS+ server first and then the locally configured enable password in case the TACACS+ server is unavailable:

```
Router#config terminal
Enter configuration commands, one per line.  End with CNTL/Z.
Router(config)#aaa new-model
Router(config)#tacacs-server host 130.218.12.10
Router(config)#tacacs-server key MyTACACSkey
Router(config)#aaa authentication enable default group tacacs+ enable
Router(config-line)#^Z
Router#
```

 Cisco provides a free Unix-based TACACS+ server that you can download from *ftp://ftp-eng.cisco.com/pub/tacacs*. This free server hasn't been updated since 1998, and if you are not comfortable using a free solution, you may want to look at Cisco's commercial access control servers.

HTTP Authentication with TACACS+

If you are running the HTTP service on your router (not recommended), you can use TACACS+ for HTTP authentication. Assuming that TACACS+ is already set up on your router, you can enable HTTP authentication through TACACS+ by:

```
Router#config terminal
Enter configuration commands, one per line.  End with CNTL/Z.
Router(config)#ip http authentication aaa
Router(config)#^Z
```

TACACS+ Authorization

In addition to authentication, TACACS+ provides very granular control over user authorization. Most configuration is done on the TACACS+ server. Using TACACS+, you can specify what a user can and cannot do. Once this information is configured on the server, you then tell the router to use the TACACS+ server to authorize every command at a specific level.

EXEC authorization

EXEC is what Cisco calls the command-line shell on its routers. You can use TACACS+ to configure which users are authorized to use the EXEC prompt to execute commands. Without access to an EXEC prompt, even users who are successfully authenticated will be unable to start a shell and will be disconnected. Most TACACS+ daemons have a default deny stance, so before you enable EXEC authorization, make sure your TACACS+ server is set up to allow at least one user EXEC access.

To use TACACS+ for EXEC authorization, enter the command:

```
Router(config)#aaa authorization exec default group tacacs+ if-authenticated
```

The final *if-authenticated* is a fail-safe that allows successfully authenticated users to start an EXEC a shell if the TACACS+ server is unavailable. This keeps you from being locked out of the router if the network or TACACS+ server is down.

Command authorization

In addition to using TACACS+ to authorize EXEC (shell) access, you can use it to specify what commands a user can and cannot run. This is done on a per-privilege-level basis, and again, most TACACS+ servers default to no authorization. Therefore, before you turn it on, make sure that the TACACS+ server is set up to allow at least one user authorization to necessary commands such as *enable* and *configure*. Command authorization is set using *aaa authorization commands*:

```
Router(conf)#aaa authorization commands 1 default group tacacs+ if-authenticated
```

This line configures the router to use the TACACS+ server to authorize all commands that are run at level 1. To configure the router to use the TACACS+ server, authorize all level 15 commands you would use:

```
Router(conf)#aaa authorization commands 15 default group tacacs+ if-authenticated
```

The final *if-authenticated* is a fail-safe that tells the router, if the TACACS+ server is unavailable, to allow authenticated users to successfully run any command at their current run level. This prevents you from being locked out of the router if the TACACS+ server is unreachable.

RADIUS Authentication

RADIUS is an access control server protocol developed by Livingston Enterprises and is documented in RFC 2865. While there are proprietary extensions to RADIUS, it is much more interoperable between different vendors than Cisco's TACACS+. However, Cisco still recommends the use of TACACS+ instead of RADIUS for the following reasons:

- RADIUS uses UDP, while TACACS+ uses TCP.
- RADIUS encrypts only the password inside access request packets, while TACACS+ encrypts the entire payload.
- RADIUS combines the authentication and authorization features, while TACACS+ provides methods to separate these two functions.
- TACACS+ has multiprotocol support built in.

However, the multivendor interoperability issue can be very compelling, and many organizations already run RADIUS authentication servers. This section details how to configure a Cisco router to authenticate to an external RADIUS server if your organization already has or chooses to use RADIUS.

To configure a router to use RADIUS authentication, perform the following steps:

1. Enable AAA with the command *aaa new-model*.

2. Tell the router what RADIUS server to use with the *radius-server host* command.

3. Tell the router what the RADIUS server key is with the *radius-server key* command.

4. Define the default AAA authentication method to be RADIUS (using the locally configured users as a backup in case the RADIUS server isn't available).

5. Configure each line to use the default AAA authentication method.

Here is an example of setting the console and VTY ports to use the RADIUS server 130.218.50.5 for authentication:

```
Router#config terminal
Enter configuration commands, one per line.  End with CNTL/Z.
Router(config)#aaa new-model
Router(config)#radius-server host 130.218.50.5
Router(config)#radius-server key MyRADIUSkey
Router(config)#aaa authentication login default group radius local
Router(config)#line con 0
Router(config-line)#login authentication default
Router(config-line)#exit
Router(config)#line vty 0 4
Router(config-line)#login authentication default
Router(config-line)#^Z
Router#
```

 IOS Versions 12.0.5(T) and later use the *aaa authentication login default group radius enable* command. Earlier versions leave out the group keyword and use the *aaa authentication login default radius enable* command.

RADIUS Enable Password

With the preceding RADIUS configuration, to set the enable password to use RADIUS for authentication, use the command:

```
aaa authentication enable default group radius enable
```

A complete configuration for only the enable password would include the following steps:

1. Enable AAA with the *aaa new-model* command.

2. Tell the router which RADIUS server to use with the *radius-server host* command.

3. Tell the router what the RADIUS server key is with *radius-server key*.

4. Configure the enable password to use the RADIUS server first and then the locally configured enable password in case the server is unavailable:

```
Router#config terminal
Enter configuration commands, one per line.  End with CNTL/Z.
Router(config)#aaa new-model
Router(config)#radius-server host 130.218.50.5
Router(config)#radius-server key MyRADIUSkey
Router(config)#aaa authentication enable default group radius enable
Router(config)#^Z
Router#
```

 RADIUS server software is very prevalent on the Internet. See the following sites for open source RADIUS software:

- *ftp://ftp.livingston.com/pub/le/radius*
- *http://www.freeradius.org*
- *http://www.radius.cistron.nl*
- *http://www.gnu.org/software/radius/radius.html*

Numerous vendors, including Cisco, also offer commercial RADIUS servers.

HTTP Authentication with RADIUS

If running the HTTP services on your router, you can use RADIUS to provide HTTP authentication. Assuming that RADIUS is already set up on your router to perform line or other authentication, the following commands will set up HTTP to use RADIUS authentication:

```
Router#config terminal
Enter configuration commands, one per line.  End with CNTL/Z.
Router(config)#ip http authentication aaa
Router(config)#^Z
Router#
```

RADIUS Authorization

Configuring RADIUS for EXEC or command authorization is very similar to the TACACS+ configuration. The only change is the RADIUS keyword instead of TACACS+. The following commands set RADIUS authorization for the EXEC commands, level 1 commands, and level 15 commands, respectively:

```
aaa authorization exec default group radius if-authenticated
aaa authorization commands 1 default group radius if-authenticated
aaa authorization commands 15 default group radius if-authenticated
```

Kerberos Authentication

Kerberos is a network authentication protocol developed by MIT. Kerberos can provide authentication only. It doesn't have the capability to perform authorization. Some sites with existing Kerberos servers use Kerberos for authentication, while using TACACS+ or RADIUS for authorization. A tutorial on Kerberos is out of the scope of this book, but see *web.mit.edu/kerberos/www* for the latest Kerberos information.

If your network uses Kerberos for authentication, the following example shows how to configure your router to use the Kerberos server for authentication. This example assumes that you are already familiar with Kerberos and have a functional Kerberos authentication server set up.

To use a Kerberos server for authentication, you must:

1. Enable AAA authentication with the *aaa new-model* command.
2. Configure Kerberos protocol support:
   a. Define the default Kerberos realm with the *kerberos local-realm* command.
   b. Specify which Kerberos server to use with the *kerberos server* command.
   c. Copy the SRVTAB from the server with the *kerberos srvtab remote* command.
   d. Enable credential forwarding with the *kerberos credential forward* command.
3. Configure the router to use Kerberos for default login authentication with locally configured usernames as a backup in case the Kerberos server isn't available.
4. Configure each line to use the default login authentication.

This example uses the Realm CISCO.COM and the Kerberos server 138.218.56.5 to configure the VTY and AUX ports to use Kerberos authentication:

```
Router#config terminal
Enter configuration commands, one per line.  End with CNTL/Z.
Router(config)#aaa new-model
Router(config)#kerberos local-realm CISCO.COM
Router(config)#kerberos server CISCO.COM 130.218.56.5
Router(config)#kerberos srvtab remote 130.218.56.5 srvtab-filename
Router(config)#kerberos credentials forward
Router(config)#aaa authentication login default krb5 local
Router(config)#line aux 0
Router(config-line)#login authentication default
Router(config-line)#exit
Router(config)#line vty 0 4
Router(config-line)#login authentication default
Router(config-line)#^Z
Router#
```

Token-Based Access Control

An authentication method that offers additional security is token-based control. With this method, each user has a smart card or token that either displays a constantly changing password or buttons that calculate a new password based on a challenge phrase. Without this card, it is impossible to authenticate yourself to the system. This two-factor authentication provides additional security by requiring an attacker to both guess the user's password and steal the smart card or token that is used to access the system.

Cisco routers don't support token-based access control directly, but there is still a way to use this authentication method. The router must be configured to use a TACACS+ or RADIUS ACS for authentication. The ACS is then configured to use smart cards or token-based access control. A word of warning, however: due to the way that HTTP performs authentication, token-based access control cannot be used.

AAA Security Checklist

This checklist summarizes the important security information presented in this chapter. A complete security checklist is provided in Appendix A. If your organization chooses to use AAA, the following checklist will help you do so securely:

- If AAA is used, when possible, use TACACS+ instead of other methods.
- If TACACS+ or RADIUS is used, then keep the configuration files secure, since TACACS+ and RADIUS keys are not obscured by the *service password-encryption* command.
- If AAA authentication is used, always set the backup method for authentication to locally configured usernames or the default privileged password and never to none.
- If AAA authorization is used and your security needs are low to medium, make sure the backup method for authorization is *if-authenticated* (to avoid being locked out of the router).
- If AAA authorization is used and you need a higher level of security, make sure there is no backup method for authorization.
- Disable HTTP access. If it must be used, make sure it uses TACACS+ or RADIUS, and not the default privileged-mode password, for authentication.
- In larger organizations that need dual-factor access control, configure the router's TACACS+ or RADIUS servers to use token-based access control.

CHAPTER 6

Warning Banners

This chapter is short, but very important. Every router should have an appropriate warning banner for all login access. These banners, however, are often thought of as pure fluff by those technically inclined. How could a warning banner serve as any protection against a hacker? What hacker is going to go away because a warning banner tells him to? It is important to remember that warning banners are not implemented to provide technical protection. They provide legal protection.

Legal Issues

Because many technicians see warning banners as worthless in the prevention of hack attacks, most systems have no banners. Even if management requires that banners be put in place, most administrators don't understand what a banner should say to provide legal protection, so even systems that have banners often include ineffectual ones.

A good warning banner has four main goals. It needs to:

- Be legally sufficient for prosecution of intruders
- Shield administrators from liability
- Warn users about monitoring or recording of system use
- Not leak information that could be useful to an attacker

Each banner should address the following issues:

Authorized users only

    The banner should specify that this system is for authorized users only. This specification keeps a hacker from claiming ignorance. While not the most effective legal strategy, with the novelty of computers and lack of case law, prosecutors are concerned enough about it that it should be included in every banner.

Official work

In addition to restricting the system to authorized users, the banner should state that the system is to be used for official work only. This statment closes the loophole of an authorized user attempting unauthorized activities.

No expectation of privacy

Every banner should explicitly state that there is no expectation of privacy when using the system. This statement is extremely important. The Electronic Communications Privacy Act makes it illegal to intercept or disclose the contents of electronic communications unless there is explicit notice that users have no expectation of privacy (or the courts grant a wiretap). Without such a warning, an administrator performing routine maintenance might be performing an illegal wiretap and violating the law.

All access and use may be monitored and/or recorded

Elaborating on the previous statement, this explicitly states that all access and use may be monitored and/or recorded. It is important to say *may be monitored* rather than *will be monitored*. Computer logs can sometimes be considered hearsay and rendered inadmissible in a court of law. If your banner says that all access *will be monitored* and you don't monitor all access, a defending attorney might be able to relegate your entire warning banner to the state of an unenforced policy and therefore render it useless in court. *May be monitored* gives you the option of choosing when to perform monitoring.

Results may be provided to appropriate officials

It is important to inform the user that any monitoring or recording that indicates abuse or criminal activity may be turned over to law enforcement or other appropriate officials.

Use implies consent

Finally, the banner should explicitly state that use of the system implies consent to all conditions laid out in the warning banner. This statement eliminates the possibility of someone claiming that they never agreed to the conditions of the banner and therefore weren't bound by them.

Without banners that display the previous information, you may cripple both your and law enforcement's ability to investigate any incidents. Additionally, if you do find the attacker, your evidence may not be admissible in court and may destroy your case. Also, many organizations like to put items in banners such as:

- Router hardware and software types
- Contact information
- Location of the router
- Name of the administrator

All of this information can be invaluable to attackers as they perform reconnaissance on your network. Anything more than the name of your organization should never be put into warning banners.

Finally, it is important to check your local legal requirements. For example, banners in Canada must include both English and French translations.

Example Banner

This example banner was provided by FBI agent Patrick Gray who works for the FBI's computer crimes division in Atlanta. It covers all of the issues mentioned earlier.

```
WARNING!!!
This system is solely for the use of authorized users for official purposes.
You have no expectation of privacy in its use and to ensure that the system
is functioning properly, individuals using this computer system are subject
to having all of their activities monitored and recorded by system
personnel.  Use of this system evidences an express consent to such
monitoring and agreement that if such monitoring reveals evidence of
possible abuse or criminal activity, system personnel may provide the
results of such monitoring to appropriate officials.
```

This is a good example of a generic banner that covers the basic needs of a banner. You may want to check with your state's attorney general to see if there are any more specifics to add that relate to your state's cybercrime laws.

 There is a cyberlegend about a case that was dismissed and a hacker let go because the system banner said *Welcome to system XYZ....* The story says that the defending attorney argued that because the system banner said *Welcome*, the hacker had been invited into the system and there was no unauthorized access. The story is fictitious, but because of the lack of cybercrime case law, it's not good to tempt fate. No matter how nice you are, don't let your system banners say *Welcome*.

Adding Login Banners

You can set four banners on Cisco routers. These banners include:

- MOTD banner
- Login banner
- AAA authentication banner
- EXEC banner

MOTD Banner

The MOTD banner sends users messages of the day and is set with the *banner motd* command. While it can be used to display the warning banner, it is generally used for more general announcements such as planned outages or system maintenance.

Login Banner

The login banner is presented each time a user attempts to log in. You definitely want to set this banner to the previous warning banner. This banner is set with the *banner login* command:

```
Router#config terminal
Enter configuration commands, one per line.  End with CNTL/Z.
Router(config)#banner login $
Enter TEXT message.  End with the character '!'.
WARNING!!!
This system is solely for the use of authorized users for official purposes.
You have no expectation of privacy in its use and to ensure that the system
is functioning properly, individuals using this computer system are subject
to having all of their activities monitored and recorded by system
personnel.  Use of this system evidences an express consent to such
monitoring and agreement that if such monitoring reveals evidence of
possible abuse or criminal activity, system personnel may provide the
results of such monitoring to appropriate officials.
$
Router(config)#^Z
Router#
```

Now when users attempt to log into the router, they see the following:

```
% telnet RouterOne
Trying RouterOne...
Connected to RouterOne.
Escape character is '^]'.

WARNING!!!
This system is solely for the use of authorized users for official purposes.
You have no expectation of privacy in its use and to ensure that the system
is functioning properly, individuals using this computer system are subject
to having all of their activities monitored and recorded by system
personnel.  Use of this system evidences an express consent to such
monitoring and agreement that if such monitoring reveals evidence of
possible abuse or criminal activity, system personnel may provide the
results of such monitoring to appropriate officials.

Username:
```

AAA Authentication Banner

If you are using AAA authentication, you can set the AAA authentication banner instead of the login banner. If both are set, both will be displayed. The AAA authentication banner is set with the *aaa authentication banner* command:

```
Router#config terminal
Enter configuration commands, one per line.  End with CNTL/Z.
Router(config)#aaa authentication banner $
Enter TEXT message.  End with the character '$'.
```

```
WARNING!!!
This system is solely for the use of authorized users for official purposes.
You have no expectation of privacy in its use and to ensure that the system
is functioning properly, individuals using this computer system are subject
to having all of their activities monitored and recorded by system
personnel.  Use of this system evidences an express consent to such
monitoring and agreement that if such monitoring reveals evidence of
possible abuse or criminal activity, system personnel may provide the
results of such monitoring to appropriate officials.
$
Router(config)#^Z
Router#
```

EXEC Banner

The EXEC banner is displayed after a user has successfully logged in and started an EXEC or shell prompt. It is a good place to provide additional notification to users and to make it even harder for them to claim that they didn't see the banner. You set the EXEC banner with the *banner exec* command:

```
Router#config terminal
Router(config)#banner exec $
Enter TEXT message.  End with the character '$'.
REMEMBER!!!
This system is solely for the use of authorized users for official purposes.
You have no expectation of privacy in its use and to ensure that the system
is functioning properly, individuals using this computer system are subject
to having all of their activities monitored and recorded by system
personnel.  Use of this system evidences an express consent to such
monitoring and agreement that if such monitoring reveals evidence of
possible abuse or criminal activity, system personnel may provide the
results of such monitoring to appropriate officials.
$
Router(config)#^Z
Router#
```

Now users see the banner before and after they log into the system:

```
% telnet RouterOne
Trying RouterOne...
Connected to RouterOne.
Escape character is '^]'.

WARNING!!!
This system is solely for the use of authorized users for official purposes.
You have no expectation of privacy in its use and to ensure that the system
is functioning properly, individuals using this computer system are subject
to having all of their activities monitored and recorded by system
personnel.  Use of this system evidences an express consent to such
monitoring and agreement that if such monitoring reveals evidence of
possible abuse or criminal activity, system personnel may provide the
results of such monitoring to appropriate officials.
```

```
Username: jdoe
Password:

REMEMBER!!!
This system is solely for the use of authorized users for official purposes.
You have no expectation of privacy in its use and to ensure that the system
is functioning properly, individuals using this computer system are subject
to having all of their activities monitored and recorded by system
personnel.  Use of this system evidences an express consent to such
monitoring and agreement that if such monitoring reveals evidence of
possible abuse or criminal activity, system personnel may provide the
results of such monitoring to appropriate officials.

Router>
```

Warning Banner Checklist

This checklist summarizes the important security information presented in this chapter. A complete security checklist is provided in Appendix A.

- Make sure every router has an appropriate warning banner that includes wording that states:
    - The router is for authorized personnel only.
    - The router is for official use only.
    - Users have no expectations of privacy.
    - All access and use may (not will) be monitored and/or recorded.
    - Monitoring and/or recording may be turned over to the appropriate authorities.
    - Use of the system implies consent to the previously mentioned conditions.
- Make sure the banner does not say *Welcome* anywhere in it.
- Make sure the banner does not include any identifying information relating to the router, the administrators, or the organization running the router.
- Check local legal requirements to make sure the banner contains all necessary language and content.
- Use the *banner login* command to display the banner every time a user attempts to log in.
- Use the *banner exec* command to display the banner a second time every time a user starts an EXEC or shell prompt.

CHAPTER 7

Unnecessary Protocols and Services

Nearly all networked systems and routers have many services automatically activated for the convenience of the administrator. These features, enabled by default, often provide attackers points of entry to gather information or gain access into the router. Since each service provides a possible access point, it is important to turn off all services that are not needed or that are security risks.

ICMP

The Internet Control Message Protocol (ICMP) enhances network functionality and is invaluable for testing network connectivity and determining network paths. No one troubleshooting a network problem would want to be without the ability to *ping* and *traceroute*. ICMP also provides incredible functionality that an attacker can manipulate to collect vast amounts of information about your routers, your network topology, and the systems on your network.

It is extremely difficult to keep a determined attacker from discovering information about any system attached to the Internet. However, the recommendations that follow will make that job harder and keep casual attackers from finding your network attractive.

ICMP MTU Discovery

Many sites choose to deny all ICMP packets into and out of their networks. This solution almost works. The only ICMP message type that causes problems when disabled is maximum transfer unit (MTU) discovery. MTU discovery optimizes the size of packets between two systems. Disabling MTU can cause severe performance problems. It can also cause sporadic problems in which small packets are allowed through, but larger ones aren't. This can cause enormous troubleshooting headaches unless the administrator understands how MTU discovery is done. To avoid these problems, you need to allow the ICMP packets responsible for MTU discovery both in and out of your network. These packets are ICMP Type 3 Code 4. On Cisco routers, you can specify the type and code directly in your ACL or use the Cisco ACL keyword *packet-too-big*.

If you want to disable all ICMP coming into your network except MTU discovery, you can add the following access list to all interfaces between your network and an external network. Here is the ACL applied to interface Serial 0/1:

```
Router#config terminal
Enter configuration commands, one per line.  End with CNTL/Z.
Router(config)#access-list 103 permit icmp any any 3 4
Router(config)#access-list 103 deny icmp any any
Router(config)#access-list 103 permit ip any any
Router(config)#interface Serial 0/1
Router(config-if)#ip access-group 103 in
Router(config-if)#^Z
Router#
```

This ACL blocks all ICMP except the Type 3 Code 4 packets needed by MTU discovery.

 Many sites also choose to allow *ping* and *traceroute* ICMP packets into their network for troubleshooting purposes. If you have one of these sites, it is important to know that *ping* uses ICMP Type 0 packets and traceroute uses ICMP Type 11. You will need to permit these packets through your ACL if you want to allow *ping* and *traceroute* functionality.

ICMP Redirects

ICMP redirects allow systems to change the way packets are passed through a network. By sending ICMP redirects, attackers can redirect all or part of your network traffic through a router of their choice, allowing them to monitor and record the traffic or even hijack sessions. On a functional network using a routing protocol, disabling ICMP redirects should have no negative impact on your networks and should help secure your routers from being manipulated by hackers.

ICMP redirects—sending

To stop your router from sending ICMP redirects, you need to enter the command *no ip redirects* under each interface. The following code stops the interface Fast Ethernet 0/0 from sending redirects:

```
Router#config terminal
Enter configuration commands, one per line.  End with CNTL/Z.
Router(config)#interface FastEthernet 0/0
Router(config-if)#no ip redirects
Router(config-if)#^Z
Router#
```

The *no ip redirects* command should be entered under each interface on every router.

ICMP redirects—receiving

To keep the router from receiving ICMP redirects, you must use access lists. The safest way is to block each interface from receiving ICMP redirects. However, on larger networks with hundreds of interfaces, this can be a daunting task. In these cases, at a minimum you need to block ICMP redirects on all router interfaces between autonomous domains (i.e., your network and one controlled by someone else). To block an interface from receiving ICMP redirects:

1. Create an ACL that blocks ICMP redirects:

   a. First it denies all ICMP redirects.

   b. Then it permits all other traffic.

2. Apply that ACL inbound on the interface:

```
Router#config terminal
Enter configuration commands, one per line.  End with CNTL/Z.
Router(config)#access-list 101 deny icmp any any redirect
Router(config)#access-list 101 permit ip any any
Router(config)#interface FastEthernet 0/0
Router(config-if)#ip access-group 101 in
Router(config-if)#^Z
Router#
```

Cisco ACLs have a default deny stance; an empty access list will deny everything. Likewise, an access list that has only an entry such as:

access-list 101 deny icmp any any redirect

will not deny just ICMP redirects (as you may suspect) but will deny everything. The moral is that you must have a permit statement somewhere in your ACL; applying an empty ACL to an interface will mean that you effectively disable that interface since it will block everything.

The ACL blocking ICMP redirects should be applied to all interfaces, if practical, and to all external interfaces, at a minimum.

The danger of blocking only ICMP redirects on interfaces between your network and external networks is that if an internal host is compromised, it can be used to send ICMP redirects and reconfigure the network paths that your systems use. If at all possible, employ ICMP redirect filtering on every router interface to eliminate this danger.

ICMP-Directed Broadcasts

Another ICMP danger is directed broadcasts. ICMP echo (*pings*) not only can be sent to a specific host, but can also be addresses to an entire network or subnet. When a single ICMP *ping* is sent to a network, then most machines on that network respond

---

to the *ping* request. This is the well-known smurf attack. An attacker sends an ICMP echo (*ping*) request to a network, but spoofs the source address to look as if it comes from a victim IP. Then tens or hundreds of machines all send back *ping* responses to the victim IP, overwhelming it. It is difficult to avoid being a victim to this type of attack, but with proper router configuration, you can prevent being a network used by an attacker. This is important for two reasons. First, hundreds of machines on your network responding to *ping* requests simultaneously can easily overwhelm your network and consume all of your bandwidth. Second, to the victim it looks as if your network is doing the attacking. You can prevent both of these problems by using the *no ip directed-broadcast* command on each router interface.

This command causes your router to block all ICMP packets sent to network or subnet addresses. To prevent your network from being a host to smurf attacks, the following example should be applied to all of your router interfaces:

```
Router#config terminal
Enter configuration commands, one per line.  End with CNTL/Z.
Router(config)#interface Serial 0/1
Router(config-if)#no ip directed broadcast
Router(config-if)#^Z
Router#
```

ICMP Mask Reply

Many ICMP functionalities have been superseded by protocols such as BOOTP and DHCP. ICMP mask reply is one of them. This ICMP type allows the router to inform hosts what the subnet mask for a network segment is. With modern protocols like DHCP, hosts should already have this information and ICMP mask replies are no longer needed. An attacker, however, may be able to use this feature to help map out the configuration of your network and routers. Therefore, unless you know that you need this feature, it is wise to disable ICMP mask replies on all routers.

Most Cisco routers default to not sending ICMP mask replies, but explicitly using this setting in the configuration file leaves no room for doubt and makes auditing the router easier. To disable ICMP mask replies, enter the *no ip mask-reply* command under each interface. The following example disables this feature for interfaces Ethernet 0/0 and Serial 0/1:

```
Router#config terminal
Enter configuration commands, one per line.  End with CNTL/Z.
Router(config)#interface Ethernet 0/0
Router(config-if)#no ip mask-reply
Router(config-if)#exit
Router(config)#interface Serial 0/1
Router(config-if)#no ip mask-reply
Router(config-if)#^Z
Router#
```

ICMP Unreachables

ICMP unreachables are sent whenever a host attempts to send a packet to a network, host, or protocol that doesn't exist or isn't supported. This is a very nice thing for remote systems to do since it immediately lets the connecting system know that its request cannot be filled. The connecting system can then error out and perform other work. When a system attempts an invalid connection but doesn't receive an ICMP unreachable message, the system then continues waiting for the remote system to respond. This waiting can last from several seconds to several minutes until the connecting system times out.

The security implications of allowing or disabling ICMP unreachables are related to an attacker scanning your router to determine what services you are running and what services might be vulnerable to attack. Many scanning methods rely on ICMP unreachable messages to concretely determine when a service is disabled. When scanning a system, ICMP unreachable messages are sent back to the attackers whenever they scan a port that is closed. The router, in effect, tells the attackers, "Sorry, this door is closed." This allows attackers to scan a system very quickly and know exactly which ports are open and which are closed. By disabling ICMP unreachables, an attacker receives no notice that the port is closed, and these types of scans take much longer to perform. While disabling ICMP unreachables works only for certain scanning methods, it does make an attacker's job a little bit harder, which is always good.

Disabling ICMP unreachables must be done on every interface with the *no ip unreachables* command. The following disables ICMP unreachables on the Fast Ethernet 0/1 and the Serial 0/0 interfaces:

```
Router#config terminal
Enter configuration commands, one per line.  End with CNTL/Z.
Router(config)#interface FastEthernet 0/1
Router(config-if)#no ip unreachables
Router(config-if)#exit
Router(config)#interface Serial 0/0
Router(config-if)#no ip unreachables
Router(config-if)#^Z
Router#
```

The *no ip unreachables* command stops each interface from sending all types of ICMP unreachable packets. While using this command helps prevent or slow down an attacker's attempt to gather information about your network and routers, it can also cause end users to experience delays when attempting to connect to an invalid network, host, or port. With ICMP unreachables enabled, users are instantly informed that they tried an invalid connection. Without ICMP unreachables, users must wait until the connection attempt times out before getting an error message. This can occasionally cause frustration among users who often attempt invalid connections.

ICMP Timestamp and Information Requests

Two other ICMP services that are usually more useful to an attacker than an administrator are the timestamp and information request packets. These ICMP types are rarely used on modern networks, but can be used by an attacker for mapping your network and possibly determining the type of routers and hosts you are running. The *timestamp* command can also provide an attacker information on the time and date set on your router. This information might help them defeat existing time-dependent security defenses.

There is no single command to disable sending responses to ICMP timestamp and information requests. You must use an ACL to keep the router from receiving these messages. To do this:

1. Create an ACL that:
    a. Denies all ICMP timestamp requests
    b. Denies all ICMP information requests
    c. Allows everything else
2. Apply the ACL to each interface or, at a minimum, interfaces between your network and one controlled by another:

    ```
    Router#config terminal
    Enter configuration commands, one per line.  End with CNTL/Z.
    Router(config)#access-list 102 deny icmp any any timestamp-request
    Router(config)#access-list 102 deny icmp any any information-request
    Router(config)#access-list 102 permit ip any any
    Router(config)#interface serial 0/0
    Router(config-if)#ip access-group 102 in
    Router(config-if)#^Z
    Router#
    ```

Source Routing

Source routing allows a packet to specify how it should be routed through a network instead of following the routers designated by the internal network's routing protocols. This can allow an attacker to bypass firewalls and intrusion detection systems. Unless you have very special circumstances that require you to enable source routing, it should be disabled on all of your routers.

The command *no ip source-route* causes the router to never honor a packet that carries source routing information:

```
Router#config terminal
Enter configuration commands, one per line.  End with CNTL/Z.
Router(config)#no ip source-route
Router(config)#^Z
Router#
```

Small Services

Depending on the IOS version you are running (Version 11.3 or prior), TCP and UDP small services may be enabled by default. These services include the echo, discard, daytime, and chargen services. These services rarely serve any purpose on a modern network and should be disabled on all routers. As a note of historical interest, one of the original denial-of-service attacks used spoofed packets to redirect one system's chargen port to another's echo port. This would consume all bandwidth between the systems as one system generated infinite characters and the other echoed these back.

Disabling these services can be done with the following commands:

```
Router#config terminal
Enter configuration commands, one per line.  End with CNTL/Z.
Router(config)#no service tcp-small-servers
Router(config)#no service udp-small-servers
Router(config)#^Z
Router#
```

Finger

The finger service can allow remote users to find out who is logged into the router. It can provide sensitive information that includes valid login names for the router. Traditionally, finger services have served hackers much more than administrators. Therefore, finger should be disabled on all routers to prevent information leakage.

Finger can be easily disabled with the *no service finger* command. This command disables the router only from replying to finger requests; it doesn't block all finger requests into your network. To do that, you would need to use an ACL that blocks TCP port 79 inbound on all external interfaces. To keep the router itself from responding to finger requests, use these commands:

```
Router#config terminal
Enter configuration commands, one per line.  End with CNTL/Z.
Router(config)#no service finger
Router(config)#^Z
```

Newer versions of IOS use the *no ip finger* command to disable finger. If the *no service finger* command doesn't work for you, try:

```
Router#config terminal
Enter configuration commands, one per line.  End with CNTL/Z.
Router(config)#no ip finger
Router(config)#^Z
```

HTTP

We have already addressed the security vulnerabilities of HTTP—namely, that all information, including login and password, is passed in clear text and that HTTP authentication cannot use one-time password or token-based authentication. For these reasons, HTTP should be disabled or severely limited. See Chapter 3 for information on disabling or restricting HTTP access.

CDP

CDP is the Cisco Discovery Protocol that provides information on remote interfaces connected to each Cisco router. It provides useful information on determining the type and configuration of a remote interface; however, it provides no information that a properly documented network will not already have recorded. CDP does, however, provide an excellent opportunity for attackers to walk from router to router and map out an entire enterprise-wide network. For this reason, accurate documentation should be kept and CDP should be disabled on all routers.

CDP can be disabled globally on a router with the *no cdp run* command:

```
Router#config terminal
Enter configuration commands, one per line.  End with CNTL/Z.
Router(config)#no cdp run
Router(config)#^Z
```

CDP can be disabled on only specific interfaces with the *no cdp enable* command:

```
Router#config terminal
Enter configuration commands, one per line.  End with CNTL/Z.
Router(config)#interface Serial 0/0
Router(config-if)#no cdp enable
Router(config-if)#^Z
Router#
```

Proxy ARP

Proxy Address Resolution Protocol (ARP) can help hosts that have no default router or gateway configured. In this case, the host simply sends an ARP on the local network and the router responds to the ARP, supplying its own MAC address as the one to use when sending to the remote system. On modern, properly configured networks where protocols such as DHCP are used, there is no reason to enable or use Proxy ARP. Attackers may be able to spoof packets to take advantage of systems performing Proxy ARP and may also be able to use a router's willingness to respond to Proxy ARP messages to gather information about your router and network.

Proxy ARP is disabled on each interface using the *no ip proxy-arp* command. The following example disables Proxy ARP on the Ethernet 0/0 and Serial 0/0 interfaces:

```
Router#config terminal
Enter configuration commands, one per line.  End with CNTL/Z.
Router(config)#interface Ethernet 0/0
Router(config-if)#no ip proxy-arp
Router(config-if)#exit
Router(config)#interface Serial 0/0
Router(config-if)#no ip proxy-arp
Router(config-if)#^Z
Router#
```

Miscellaneous

Many services may also be enabled by default, but are not needed. Good security means shutting off everything that is not required, so unless you know you require these services, they should be disabled. These services include:

- BootP
- DNS
- Network autoloading of configuration files
- PAD—packet assembly/disassembly
- IP classless

The following commands disable these services:

```
Router#config terminal
Enter configuration commands, one per line.  End with CNTL/Z.
Router(config)#no ip bootp server
Router(config)#no ip name-server
Router(config)#no service config
Router(config)#no boot network
Router(config)#no service pad
Router(config)#no ip classless
Router(config)#^Z
```

 By default, Cisco routers come with DNS enabled, but no nameserver configured. This causes Cisco routers to use broadcasts for DNS queries. In the best case, this causes annoying delays at the EXEC prompt. In the worst case, an attacker can respond to these broadcast DNS queries with false information that could fool your router into using the wrong hosts. If you don't want to use DNS, use the *ip name-server* command to statically configure DNS servers on your routers (to avoid using broadcast DNS queries).

SNMP

SNMP can often be a gold mine to an attacker. SNMP is usually enabled by default and uses the default access strings *public* and *private*. Many administrators do not disable SNMP and also do not change from the defaults. This lets attackers use SNMP to gather almost any information about your router that they want and often lets them use SNMP to reconfigure your router. Disable SNMP if it is not needed, and severely restrict its access if it is enabled. See Chapter 8 for details on SNMP security.

Unnecessary Protocols and Services Checklist

This checklist summarizes the important security information presented in this chapter. A complete security checklist is provided in Appendix A.

- Disable the following services on every interface on every router:
    - Disable sending ICMP redirects with the *no ip redirects* command.
    - Disable ICMP broadcasts with the *no ip directed-broadcast* command.
    - Disable ICMP mask replies with the *no ip mask-reply* command.
    - Disable ICMP unreachables with the *no ip unreachables* command.
    - Disable Proxy ARP with the *no ip proxy-arp* command.
- Disable CDP globally with the *no cdp run* command or disable it on each interface with the *no cdp enable* command.
- Disable source routing with the *no ip source-route* command.
- Disable small services with the *no service tcp-small-servers* and the *no service udp-small-servers* commands.
- Disable Finger with the *no service finger* command.
- Severely restrict incoming ICMP packets using an appropriate ACL. (Ideally, only MTU discovery is allowed between your internal network and external networks.)
- Disable miscellaneous services such as *BOOTP*, PAD, configuration autoloading, and DNS.
- Disable or secure HTTP access (see Chapter 3).
- Disable or secure SNMP access (see Chapter 8).

CHAPTER 8
SNMP Security

The Simple Network Management Protocol (SNMP) is an extremely useful protocol for monitoring and managing TCP/IP networks. Most networked systems come with at least a basic SNMP service enabled by default, allowing you to collect information about your network remotely. If write access is enabled, SNMP can also be used to configure devices on your network remotely.

Since read-only SNMP is enabled by default on many systems, it is an attacker's dream. An attacker can use SNMP to map out your entire network, find out MAC and IP address binding, and even find out exactly what hardware you are using and what software versions you are running. At attacker can then use that information to search vulnerability databases and analyze your network for vulnerable trust relationships.

The following example shows just how much information an attacker can gain about your router and network through unsecured SNMP. Using the Net-SNMP *snmpwalk* program to get the routers system information through SNMP, you see:

```
% snmpwalk -v1 RouterOne public system
system.sysDescr.0 = Cisco Internetwork Operating System Software
IOS (tm) C2600 Software (C2600-DO3S-M), Version 12.0(5)T1,  RELEASE SOFTWARE (fc1)
Copyright (c) 1986-1999 by cisco Systems, Inc.
Compiled Tue 17-Aug-99 13:18 by cmong
system.sysContact.0 = Jane Doe <jdoe@routerone.edu>  - Office BB 983 - x3334
system.sysName.0 = RouterOne
system.sysLocation.0 = Building A Basement - Closet 936
```

You now have the exact hardware and software versions of this router, contact information, the router's name, and its physical location.

This is only the tip of the iceberg; from a full *snmpwalk* you get a list of each interface on this router, what types of interfaces they are, and their physical and network addresses. Additionally, you can get a complete list of this router's routing tables, ARP tables, and even how long the router has been up since the last boot. All of this information is a gold mine for someone trying to break into your network. With this information, an attacker often understands your network better than you do.

Net-SNMP is a suite of tools that includes an open source SNMP server and can be found at *http://net-snmp.sourceforge.net*. For more information on SNMP in general, see *http://www.simpleweb.org*.

SNMP Versions

Three main versions of SNMP are in use today. The oldest and most widely used is SNMP Version 1. The second, SNMP v2c, has a few improvements over SNMP v1, but uses the same methods for security. SNMP v3 has enhanced security measures that allow the use of SNMP in environments requiring additional security.

SNMP Version 1

SNMP v1 gained popularity in the early 1990s and quickly became the standard way to monitor network devices remotely. It was quickly discovered that SNMP v1 had some inherent security flaws, but at the time, because it was so useful and e-commerce was in its infancy, few worried about these flaws. As the Internet progressed and more servers containing sensitive information were attached, the security flaw of SNMP v1 became more problematic.

A key security flaw in SNMP v1 is that the only authentication available is through a community string. Think of a community string as a group password—anyone who knows the community string is allowed access. Adding to this problem is the fact that all SNMP v1 packets are passed unencrypted across the network. Therefore, anyone who can sniff a single SNMP packet now has the community string needed to get access.

SNMP Version 2c

SNMP v2 was the first attempt to fix these security flaws. However, the members of the Internet Engineering Task Force (IETF) subcommittee responsible for the v2 standard had trouble agreeing on the security and administrative aspects of the protocol. Therefore, SNMP v2 never really took off. The only prevalent version of SNMP v2 today is SNMP v2c, which contains SNMP v2 protocol enhancements, but leaves out the security features that no one could agree on. The *c* designates v2c as being "community based," which means that it uses the same authentication mechanism as v1—community strings.

SNMP Version 3

SNMP v3 was the next attempt to fix the security vulnerabilities inherent to SNMP v1 and v2c. SNMP v3 provides many security enhancement, but is currently still a draft-standard and not yet a full standard. This has kept many vendors from implementing SNMP v3 or caused them to develop proprietary versions of SNMP v3. The key security additions to SNMP v3 are that it:

- Can use MD5 or SHA hashes for authentication
- Can encrypt the entire packet
- Can guarantee message integrity

SNMP v3 allows you to choose to use no authentication and no encryption (*NoAuthNoPriv*), authentication but no encryption (*AuthNoPriv*), or authentication and encryption (*AuthPriv*). See Table 8-1 for a comparison of SNMP version features.

Table 8-1. Cisco router SNMP version comparison

Version	Authentication	Encryption	Function
v1	Community strings	None	Uses community string for authentication. Packet is passed in clear text.
v2	Community strings	None	Uses community string for authentication. Packet is passed in clear text.
v3 (NoAuthNoPriv)	Username	None	Uses username for authentication. Packet is passed in clear text.
v3 (AuthNoPriv)	MD5 or SHA	None	Uses HMAC-MD5 or HMAC-SHA for authentication. Remaining packet is passed in clear text.
v3 (AuthPriv)	MD5 or SHA	DES	Uses HMAC-MD5 or HMAC-SHA for authentication. Entire packet is encrypted.

If you are new to SNMP, start with SNMP v1 to learn how SNMP works. On smaller, low-risk networks, SNMP v1 or v2c can be used regularly if community strings are changed and access is restricted to specific IP addresses. On larger, more sensitive networks, however, It is recommended that you use either SNMP v3 with encryption and authentication or IPSec to encrypt the SNMP v1 traffic between your routers and management stations.

Despite the benefits of SNMP v3, you will face some significant hurdles in its implementation. First, very few vendors who sell software for SNMP management stations currently support SNMP v3. Second, SNMP v3 uses Data Encryption Standard (DES) encryption, which many security professionals consider to be too weak to be effective for high-security networks.

Securing SNMP v1 and v2c

Since SNMP v1 and v2c use the same community-based authentication methods, they are grouped together on Cisco routers. You either enable both or neither.

Enabling SNMP v1 and v2c

First, for security reasons, it is strongly recommended that you disable SNMP v1 and v2c on all your routers. SNMP v3 is much better suited for secure enterprise-wide use. However, if SNMP v1 or v2 must be used, then the following security precautions must be taken:

- Do not enable read/write access unless absolutely necessary.
- Choose secure (difficult to guess) community strings. Ideally, you would use different community strings on each router, but this usually isn't practical due to the way most SNMP network management servers function.
- Limit all SNMP access to specific IP addresses using ACLs.
- Limit SNMP output with views.

The rest of this section discusses how to accomplish these tasks and make SNMP v1 and v2c as secure as possible.

Community strings

When enabling SNMP v1 and v2c, two levels of privilege can be configured. The first is read-only; the second, read/write. Read-only allows remote users to use SNMP to get statistics and information from the router, but allows no changes to made to the router itself. Read/write access allows remote users to read information from the router and reconfigure the router.

Community strings are the basis for SNMP v1 and v2c authentication. Unless additional IP-based restrictions are configured, anyone who knows the community string can access the router. There are two serious repercussions to this. First, most network devices ship with a default read-only community string, *public*. This default community string is well known and should never be used. The default community string for read/write access is *private*. Again, this string is well known, and if read/write access is enabled, it should be changed. The same rules for choosing a good password apply to choosing a good community string. See the "Strong Passwords" section of Chapter 4 for information on choosing strong community strings. Next, with SNMP v1 and v2c, the community string is passed in clear text across the network. This makes their secure use extremely limited since anyone with a sniffer can obtain your community strings and therefore access your routers. If you decide to use SNMP v1 or v2c, make sure your organization can live with these risks. Many organizations choose to use read-only SNMP v1 or v2c, restricted by IP address to specific internal machines, and totally block SNMP access on all external router interfaces.

Read-only access

To configure read-only SNMP v1 and v2c access, use the *snmp-server community* command followed by a community string and the *RO* keyword:

```
Router#config terminal
Enter configuration commands, one per line.  End with CNTL/Z.
Router(config)#snmp-server community UnGuessableStringReadOnly RO
Router(config)#^Z
```

Read/write access

To configure read/write SNMP v1 and v2c access, use the *snmp-server* command followed by a different community string and the *RW* keyword:

```
Router#config terminal
Enter configuration commands, one per line.  End with CNTL/Z.
Router(config)#snmp-server community UnGuessableStringWriteable RW
Router(config)#^Z
```

Disabling SNMP v1 and v2c

Disabling SNMP can be done entirely with the command *no snmp-server*. Use the following example to specifically disable read/write or read-only access.

Using the *no snmp-server* command disables all SNMP versions on your router. However, until the system is rebooted, it holds the previous SNMP configuration in memory. The configuration is inactive, but if you reenable SNMP, this previous configuration information can sometimes be reloaded into the running configuration. This can be especially tricky in cases when you have SNMP v1 and v2c enabled; use the *no snmp-server* command to disable SNMP and then configure SNMP v3. Make sure that your previous SNMP v1 and v2c configurations have not been restored without your knowledge.

Disabling read-only access

To disable read-only SNMP v1 and v2c access, explicitly use the *no snmp-server community* command followed by the read-only community string and the *RO* keyword. If your read-only community string is *UnGuessableStringReadOnly*, you would input:

```
Router#config terminal
Enter configuration commands, one per line.  End with CNTL/Z.
Router(config)#no snmp-server community UnGuessableStringReadOnly RO
Router(config)#^Z
```

Disabling read/write access

To disable read/write SNMP v1 and v2c access, explicitly use the no *snmp-server* community command followed by the read/write community string and the *RW* keyword. If your read/write community string is *UnGuessableStringWritable*, you would type:

```
Router#config terminal
Enter configuration commands, one per line.  End with CNTL/Z.
Router(config)#no snmp-server community UnGuessableStringWriteable RW
Router(config)#^Z
```

Limiting SNMP v1 and v2c Access by IP

You should always limit SNMP access to only a few specific IP addresses; this is especially true when using SNMP v1 and v2c. To do this:

1. Create an appropriate ACL.
2. Configure read-only or read/write access to use that ACL.

Read-only access

Restricting read-only access by IP address uses the same command as enabling read-only SNMP, with one addition: you append the number of ACL. To restrict read-only SNMP access to the IP addresses 130.218.10.8 and 130.218.14.7, you would type:

```
Router#config terminal
Enter configuration commands, one per line.  End with CNTL/Z.
Router(config)#access-list 6 permit 130.218.10.8
Router(config)#access-list 6 permit 130.218.14.7
Router(config)#access-list 6 deny any
Router(config)#snmp-server community UnGuessableStringReadOnly RO 6
Router(config)#^Z
```

Read/write access

Restricting read/write access is almost the same as the previous example with the exception of the *RW* keyword in place or *RO*. Restricting read/write access to the same IPs as before—130.218.10.8 and 130.218.14.7—would require:

```
Router#config terminal
Enter configuration commands, one per line.  End with CNTL/Z.
Router(config)#access-list 8 permit 130.218.10.8
Router(config)#access-list 8 permit 130.218.14.7
Router(config)#access-list 8 deny any
Router(config)#snmp-server community UnGuessableStringWriteable RW 8
Router(config)#^Z
```

Since the IPs in both examples are the same, you don't have to create a separate ACL and can use the same ACL, number 6, to restrict both read-only and read/write access.

Read-only SNMP access allows an attacker to see how your router and network are configured. While this is extremely valuable information, it doesn't come close to what an attacker can do with read/write access. Read/write access gives an attacker complete control over your router. Using *SNMPset,* an attacker can completely reconfigure your router, including resetting your passwords, disabling ACLs, and redirecting traffic.

SNMP Read/Write and TFTP

There is a major security risk associated with SNMP read/write access that involves TFTP. When SNMP read/write access is enabled, attackers can use SNMP to cause the router to either TFTP its configuration file to them, or even have the router load a new configuration from an arbitrary TFTP server. To avoid this problem, it is important to use the *snmp-server tftp-server-list* command to limit what IP addresses are allowed to use TFTP servers via SNMP.

The following example shows how to use an ACL to restrict SNMP-controlled TFTP access to the IP 130.8.4.9:

```
RouterOne#config terminal
Enter configuration commands, one per line.  End with CNTL/Z.
RouterOne(config)#access-list 98 permit host 130.8.4.9
RouterOne(config)#access-list 98 deny any
RouterOne(config)#snmp-server tftp-server-list 98
RouterOne(config)#^Z
```

If you don't use TFTP, then create an empty ACL and apply it. Since ACLs are default deny, this will keep anyone from using SNMP and TFTP to manipulate your router.

 Cisco routers have a command that enables them to be rebooted through SNMP remotely—*snmp-server system-shutdown.* This command is disabled by default and should not be turned on. The potential for abuse greatly outweighs the utility of this feature.

Limiting SNMP v1 and v2c Access with Views

Another way to help secure SNMP v1 and v2c is to limit what information remote systems can see. This is extremely useful when only specific information is needed through SNMP. To use views:

1. Create a view specifying what information is allowed to be seen using the *snmp-server view* command.

2. Create a new community string with the *snmp-server community* command that specifies the view we created previously.

The SNMP MIB defines what information you can retrieve or set through SNMP. Standard MIBs, such as MIB-II, are supported by every network device, and proprietary MIBs are only for specific products. MIBs consist of a treelike structure and are organized with Object Identifiers (OID). Knowing the OID lets you access the specific information you are looking for. For more information on MIBs and OIDs, see *http://www.simpleweb.org*.

The *snmp-server view* command takes three arguments. The first is the name you want to call the view, then the table name or MIB Object Identifier (OID), and finally the keyword *include* or *exclude*. If you know SNMP well, you can create advanced lists by using the OID numbers. If you're not an SNMP expert, you can use table names such as IP, ICMP, TCP, SYSTEM, INTERFACES, and so on. Like access lists, the default policy of a view is to deny access and not return any data. The following example creates a view called *tcp-only* that allows access to the MIB objects only under the TCP table:

```
Router#config terminal
Enter configuration commands, one per line.  End with CNTL/Z.
Router(config)#snmp-server view tcp-only tcp include
Router(config)#snmp-server community TcpOnlyCommunityString view tcp-only
Router(config)#^Z
```

Now, when you attempt to get SNMP information from the router using the *TcpOnlyCommunityString* command, you see only the information in the TCP table:

```
% snmpwalk -v1 RouterOne TcpOnlyCommunityString
tcp.tcpRtoAlgorithm.0 = vanj(4)
tcp.tcpRtoMin.0 = 300 milliseconds
tcp.tcpRtoMax.0 = 60000 milliseconds
tcp.tcpMaxConn.0 = -1
tcp.tcpActiveOpens.0 = 0
tcp.tcpPassiveOpens.0 = 2
tcp.tcpAttemptFails.0 = 0
tcp.tcpEstabResets.0 = 0
tcp.tcpCurrEstab.0 = Gauge: 1
tcp.tcpInSegs.0 = 3698
tcp.tcpOutSegs.0 = 2549
tcp.tcpRetransSegs.0 = 1
tcp.tcpConnTable.tcpConnEntry.tcpConnState.130.218.9.50.23.130.218.59.1.64880 =
established(5)
tcp.tcpConnTable.tcpConnEntry.tcpConnLocalAddress.130.218.9.50.23.130.218.9.41.64880
= IpAddress: 130.218.59.250
tcp.tcpConnTable.tcpConnEntry.tcpConnLocalPort.130.218.9.50.23.130.218.9.41.64880 =
23
tcp.tcpConnTable.tcpConnEntry.tcpConnRemAddress.130.218.9.50.23.130.218.9.41.64880 =
IpAddress: 130.218.59.41
tcp.tcpConnTable.tcpConnEntry.tcpConnRemPort.130.218.9.50.23.130.218.9.41.64880 =
64880
tcp.tcpInErrs.0 = 0
tcp.tcpOutRsts.0 = 0
End of MIB
```

Table 8-2 contains some useful keywords for creating views.

Table 8-2. SNMP keywords

SNMP MIB keyword	Reported information
System	Information about the system, including hardware, software, contact, and location
Interfaces	Information about every interface on the system, including packets in, packets out, errors, etc.
at	The ARP table mappings
Ip	IP statistics and tables including the routing tables
Icmp	ICMP statistics
tcp	TCP statistics, including the connection tables with port numbers
udp	UDP statistics, including the connection tables with port numbers
snmp	SNMP statistics

Finally, one of the most useful features of SNMP views is its ability to limit SNMP write access in addition to limiting read-only access.

> SNMP v3 is not yet a full standard. Many vendors have not implemented it or have implemented incompatible versions of SNMP v3. One way to get the advantages of SNMP v3 authentication and encryption while still using SNMP v1 or SNMP v2 is to use IPSec between the router and the SNMP management station. See Chapter 3 for more information on configuring IPSec.

Securing SNMP v3

In relation to security, the major change in SNMP v3 is the ability to authenticate and encrypt SNMP packets. This ability allows you to use SNMP securely across untrustworthy networks. The current disadvantage of SNMP v3, however, is that it is not supported on all network devices or all network management stations. Cisco routers running IOS 12.0(3)T and above include SNMP v3 support.

The three levels of SNMP v3 security are no authentication and no encryption, authentication and no encryption, and authentication and encryption. SNMP v3 specifies these levels as *NoAuthNoPriv*, *AuthNoPriv*, and *AuthPriv*, respectively. Table 8-3 shows the Cisco keywords that map to these security levels.

Table 8-3. SNMP security and Cisco keywords

SNMP security keyword	Cisco keyword
NoAuthNoPriv	Noauth
AuthNoPriv	Auth
AuthPriv	Priv

Whenever you see a router command that specifies *priv* as the SNMP v3 security level, it really indicates both authentication and encryption.

No Authentication/No Encryption

The least-secure method of SNMP v3 uses no authentication and no encryption. This is referred to as *NoAuthNoPriv*. With this type of SNMP v3 packet, the only type of access control is through a username. To configure SNMP v3 *NoAuthNoPriv* access on a router, you must:

1. Configure an SNMP v3 group that specifies no authentication with the *snmp-server group* command and the *noauth* keyword.

2. Create an SNMP v3 user in that group with the *snmp-server user* command.

The *snmp-server group* command can take many different arguments, depending on how you want the group set up. The first two arguments indicate the name of the group and the SNMP version of the group. Additional arguments can specify access lists, restricted views, or authentication and encryption methods. In the following example, the *v3* indicates SNMP v3 and *noauth* indicates that no authentication or encryption is to be used.

The *snmp-server user* command also takes various arguments. The first three are the name of the user, the name of the group that user belongs to, and the SNMP version that user runs. Additional arguments specify authentication and encryption information:

```
Router#config terminal
Enter configuration commands, one per line.  End with CNTL/Z.
Router(config)#snmp-server group NoAuthGroup v3 noauth
Router(config)#snmp-server user MyUser1 NoAuthGroup v3
Router(config)#^Z
```

Now you can use unauthenticated and unencrypted SNMP to access information about the router by specifying user *MyUser1*:

```
% snmpwalk -v 3 -l NoAuthNoPriv -u MyUser1 RouterOne
system.sysDescr.0 = Cisco Internetwork Operating System Software
IOS (tm) C2600 Software (C2600-IS56I-M), Version 12.1(1), RELEASE SOFTWARE (fc1)
Copyright (c) 1986-2000 by cisco Systems, Inc.
Compiled Wed 15-Mar-00 03:45 by cmong
system.sysObjectID.0 = OID: enterprises.9.1.208
system.sysUpTime.0 = Timeticks: (888383) 2:28:03.83
system.sysContact.0 =
system.sysName.0 = RouterOne.kennesaw.edu
[ cut ]
```

Using no authentication and no encryption (*NoAuthNoPriv*) means that you are still vulnerable to someone sniffing your username and gaining SNMP access. If you are going to use SNMP v3, it is recommended that you use both authentication and encryption (*AuthPriv*).

Authentication/No Encryption

The level of protection above a simple username is authentication. This is the *AuthNoPriv* level in which users are securely authenticated, but packets are still passed unencrypted. This level allows you to specify a different username and password for every user who requires SNMP access, giving you the accountability that you lack when using just a community string.

To configure SNMP v3 authentication, you must:

1. Create an SNMP v3 group that is configured to use authentication with the *snmp-server group* command and the *auth* keyword.

2. Create an SNMP v3 user in that group and give that user an authentication method and password. The *auth* keyword, followed by an authentication method, here *md5*, is followed by the SNMP v3 user password:

```
Router#config terminal
Enter configuration commands, one per line.  End with CNTL/Z.
Router(config)#snmp-server group AuthGroup v3 auth
Router(config)#snmp-server user MyUser2 AuthGroup v3 auth md5 MyAuthPassword
Router(config)#^Z
```

Now you can access the SNMP v3 information only by successfully authenticating yourself with the username *MyUser2* and the password *MyAuthPassword*. Even though you are authenticating, you are still not using encryption and are at the *AuthNoPriv* level:

```
% snmpwalk -v 3 -u MyUser2 -l AuthNoPriv -A MyAuthPassword RouterOne
system.sysDescr.0 = Cisco Internetwork Operating System Software
IOS (tm) C2600 Software (C2600-IS56I-M), Version 12.1(1), RELEASE SOFTWARE (fc1)
Copyright (c) 1986-2000 by cisco Systems, Inc.
Compiled Wed 15-Mar-00 03:45 by cmong
system.sysObjectID.0 = OID: enterprises.9.1.208
system.sysUpTime.0 = Timeticks: (1008588) 2:48:05.88
system.sysContact.0 =
system.sysName.0 = RouterOne.kennesaw.edu
[ cut ]
```

Authentication/Encryption

Finally, there is the *AuthPriv* level, which uses both strong authentication and encryption. This level is the most appropriate level to use on secure networks. SNMP v3 requires separate passwords for authentication and encryption for each username. To configure a user to use authentication and encryption:

1. Create a group that is configured to use both authentication and encryption using the *snmp-server group* command and the *priv* keyword.

2. Create a user in that group to whom you assign separate authentication and encryption passwords using the *snmp-server user* command and the *priv*

keyword. The *auth* keyword is followed by the authentication method, *md5*, and the *priv* keyword is followed by the encryption type, *des56*:

```
Router#config terminal
Enter configuration commands, one per line.  End with CNTL/Z.
Router(config)#snmp-server group AuthPrivGroup v3 priv
Router(config)#snmp-server user MyUser3 AuthPrivGroup v3 auth md5 AuthPass \
priv des56 PrivPass
Router(config)#^Z
```

When you request SNMP v3 information from the router, you must use the correct username, authentication password, and encryption password. When you do, all communication is encrypted:

```
% snmpwalk -v 3 -u MyUser3 -l authpriv -A AuthPass -X PrivPass RouterOne
system.sysDescr.0 = Cisco Internetwork Operating System Software
IOS (tm) C2600 Software (C2600-IS56I-M), Version 12.1(1), RELEASE SOFTWARE (fc1)
Copyright (c) 1986-2000 by cisco Systems, Inc.
Compiled Wed 15-Mar-00 03:45 by cmong
system.sysObjectID.0 = OID: enterprises.9.1.208
system.sysUpTime.0 = Timeticks: (1008588) 2:48:05.88
system.sysContact.0 =
system.sysName.0 = RouterOne.kennesaw.edu
[ cut ]
```

 SNMP v3 uses an identification number called the *engineID*. This number is set on your router automatically. Both authentication and encryption functions rely on this number not changing. If you purposefully or accidentally change your *engineID* number, you will disable your current users and groups and will need to delete and re-create them.

Limiting SNMP v3 Access by IP

You can also use ACLs with SNMP v3 to further enhance your security. You can specify an access list at the group or user level. In either case, add the keyword *access* followed by the restricting ACL to any of the preceding *snmp-server group* or *user* commands.

The following example:

- Creates an ACL that restricts access to the systems 130.218.9.12 and 130.218.9.14 with the *access-list* command
- Creates an SNMP v3 group called *Trusted* that uses the ACL to restrict access for all members of that group with the *snmp-server group* command and the *access* keyword
- Creates the users Jeff and Sara inside the *Trusted* group with the *snmp-server user* command

```
Router#config terminal
Enter configuration commands, one per line.  End with CNTL/Z.
Router(config)#access-list 5 permit 130.218.9.12
```

```
Router(config)#access-list 5 permit 130.218.9.14
Router(config)#access-list 5 deny any
Router(config)#snmp-server group Trusted v3 auth access 5
Router(config)#snmp-server user jeff Trusted v3 auth md5 JeffsPass
Router(config)#snmp-server user sara Trusted v3 auth md5 SarasPass
Router(config)#^Z
```

Limiting IP addresses on a per-user basis is similar:

1. Create an ACL that limits access based on IP with the *access-list* command. This example uses 130.218.12.5 and 130.218.6.3.

2. Create a group that specifies authentication and encryption information with the *snmp-server group* command.

3. Create users in this group and specify the ACL for each user with the *snmp-server user* command and the *access* keyword. The following example restricts Thomas to the IP 130.218.12.5 and Abigail to the IP 130.218.6.3:

```
Router#config terminal
Enter configuration commands, one per line.  End with CNTL/Z.
Router(config)#access-list 6 permit 130.218.12.5
Router(config)#access-list 6 deny any
Router(config)#access-list 7 permit 130.218.6.3
Router(config)#access-list 7 deny any
Router(config)#snmp-server group AdminGroup v3 auth
Router(config)#snmp-server user thomas AdminGroup v3 auth md5 TsPass access 6
Router(config)#snmp-server user abigail AdminGroup v3 auth md5 AsPass access 7
Router(config)#^Z
```

Limiting SNMP v3 Output with Views

Views can be applied to SNMP v3 groups, but not directly to users. The process is similar to creating views for SNMP v1 and v2c. When creating a group that restricts information with views, use the *read* or *write* keywords to indicate whether the view applies to read-only access or read/write access.

1. Create a view restricting access to SNMP information with the *snmp-server view* command.

2. Create a group to which you apply that view with the *snmp-server group* command. You can apply the view to read or write access. This example uses the *read* keyword so the view is applied to read-only access for this group.

3. Create users inside the group with the *snmp-server user* command and they will be restricted by that group's view.

The following example restricts all the members of group *IpOnly* to viewing the IP information (but nothing else):

```
Router#config terminal
Enter configuration commands, one per line.  End with CNTL/Z.
Router(config)#snmp-server view IpOnlyView ip include
Router(config)#snmp-server group IpOnly v3 noauth read IpOnlyView
```

```
Router(config)#snmp-server user heather IpOnly v3
Router(config)#^Z
```

Now when Heather uses SNMP v3 to access the router, she will only get information about the IP protocol.

Finally, you can combine views and access lists. This example creates a group that restricts access to the single IP 130.218.250.5 and allows read-only access to the interface information and nothing more:

```
Router#config terminal
Enter configuration commands, one per line.  End with CNTL/Z.
Router(config)#access-list 10 permit 130.218.250.5
Router(config)#access-list 10 deny any
Router(config)#snmp-server view IntView interface include
Router(config)#snmp-server group IntGroup v3 auth read IntView access 10
Router(config)#snmp-server user bob IntGroup v3 auth md5 BobsPass
Router(config)#^Z
```

SNMP Management Servers

Finally, with all this effort to secure the SNMP access on the routers, you can't forget the SNMP management station. Just as storing your router configurations on an insecure box can lead to a compromise, leaving your SNMP management server unsecured is an invitation for attack.

By its very nature, the SNMP management server must have the SNMP information for every system that it monitors. This information includes IP addresses, SNMP community strings, SNMP v3 usernames, and authentication and encryption passwords. Additionally, SNMP management servers must also have access to query each system, meaning that you must allow the server through your ACLs. Therefore, if an SNMP management server is compromised, an attacker has just gained access information for every system monitored on your network and also a platform from which to perform additional monitoring and attacks (since the SNMP management server will necessarily have SNMP access to the routers).

Therefore, in addition to hardening your routers, you must make sure that the SNMP management station is also secured.

SNMP Security Checklist

This checklist summarizes the important security information presented in this chapter. A complete security checklist is provided in Appendix A.

- Disable SNMP, if it is not needed.
- Use different community or authentication strings for each router, if possible. (This often become unmanageable.)

- Make sure community strings and passwords are well chosen and not easily guessed.
- Restrict all SNMP access to specific hosts through ACLs.
- Restrict all SNMP output through the use of views.
- Disable read/write SNMP access unless absolutely necessary.
- If SNMP read/write access is configured, use the *snmp-server tftp-server-list* command to restrict SNMP-controlled TFTP transfers.
- Disable SNMP v1 and v2c in favor of SNMP v3.
- Under SNMP v3:
  - Make sure that SNMP v1 and v2c are disabled.
  - Use both authentication and encryption (*AuthPriv*) on your routers.
  - Use views to limit SNMP access to information.
- Secure all SNMP Management Servers.

CHAPTER 9

Secure Routing and Antispoofing

This chapter covers both antispoofing and securing the routing protocol your routers use to exchange information. Antispoofing filters prevent external users from sending forged packets that act as if they come from your internal network. Many security controls use a packet's source IP address to allow or deny access. By sending spoofed packets that look as if they originated on your internal network, attackers can manipulate or bypass these security controls.

Your routers use routing protocols to exchange information. This information is used to determine what direction a router will send a packet once it is received. A functional network requires correct routing information, so, minimally, an attacker can cause a denial-of-service (DoS) attack by inserting false routing information into your routers. A far more damaging attack can involve having all of your network traffic relayed through another system, possibly one controlled by the attacker or one that allows him to bypass your firewall and intrusion detection systems. Protecting how routers exchange routing information is necessary to prevent such dangers.

Antispoofing

Antispoofing filters are usually implemented to protect the networks behind routers, but they are equally important in protecting the routers themselves. These filters keep people from attempting to spoof connections to your routers. They also prevent numerous attacks that, while not directed at the router, must pass through the router and can overwhelm it with excessive traffic.

This chapter will cover both inbound and outbound filters using traditional ACLs and Cisco's newer unicast reverse packet forwarding feature. Finally, since filtering can cause some performance degradation, the checklist ends with brief descriptions of methods used to reduce the performance impact of antispoofing filters.

Ingress and Egress Filtering

Ingress and egress refer to filters applied to packets traveling into and out of a network, respectively. Ingress refers to packets coming from an external network—like the Internet—into your network, and egress refers to packets leaving your network and going to an external network. Your site needs to implement both types of filters.

Since ingress and egress filters relate to packets entering or leaving your network, they should be applied at the edges of your network—anywhere you connect to a network controlled by another.

Ingress

Ingress filters make sure that packets entering your network do not claim to be from your network. Assume that your network is 130.218.0.0/16. All IPs leaving your network should have a source address of 130.218.x.x. Additionally, no packets coming into your network should have a source address of 130.218.x.x. A packet from an external network with a source address of 130.18.x.x stems from either a misconfiguration or an attacker attempting to send spoofed packets into your network. Either way, packets from external networks claiming to have a source address of your internal network—138.18.x.x, in this example—are dangerous and should be dropped.

To drop these packets:

1. Create an ACL that:
    a. Denies all packets coming from the Internet claiming to have originated from the internal network
    b. Permits all other packets
2. Apply that ACL, in the inbound direction, to the router interface that connects to the external network.

Using the interface Serial 0 and the internal network 130.18.00/16, the code would look like:

```
Router#config terminal
Enter configuration commands, one per line.  End with CNTL/Z.
Router(config)#access-list 15 deny 130.18.0.0 0.0.255.255
Router(config)#access-list 15 permit any
Router(config)#interface Serial 0/0
Router(config-if)#ip access-group 15 in
Router(config-if)#^Z
```

If you have more than one network numbering scheme inside your internal network, you would extend the deny statements to include all of your internal networks. For example, if your internal network consisted of the following networks:

```
203.2.4.0/24
199.10.4.0/27
215.6.45.0/24
```

your ingress ACL would look like:

```
access-list 15 deny 203.2.4.0 0.0.0.255
access-list 15 deny 199.10.4.0 0.0.0.31
access-list 15 deny 215.6.45.0 0.0.0.255
access-list 15 permit any
```

Finally, to fully protect your router and network, you should apply the ingress filter to all interfaces that attach to an external network.

Reserved and private networks

Antispoofing filters also need to include rules that filter out any packets that claim to come from reserved and private networks. The standard list includes the loopback address, the broadcast address, multicast networks, and networks defined in RFC 1918 as reserved:

- 127.0.0.0/8
- 10.0.0.0/8
- 172.16.0.0/12
- 192.168.0.0/16
- 224.0.0.0/4
- 240.0.0.0/5
- 255.255.255.255/32

Adding these filters to our previous example (in which the internal networks were assumed to be 203.2.4.0/24, 199.10.4.0/27, and 215.6.45.0/24), you get the following ACL:

```
access-list 15 deny 203.2.4.0 0.0.0.255
access-list 15 deny 199.10.4.0 0.0.0.31
access-list 15 deny 215.6.45.0 0.0.0.255
access-list 15 deny 127.0.0.0 0.255.255.255
access-list 15 deny 10.0.0.0 0.255.255.255
access-list 15 deny 172.16.0.0 0.15.255.255
access-list 15 deny 192.168.0.0 0.0.255.255
access-list 15 deny 224.0.0.0 15.255.255.255
access-list 15 deny 240.0.0.0 7.255.255.255
access-list 15 permit any
```

 Some administrators like to go all out with their spoofing filters. The site *http://www.liquifried.com/docs/security/reservednets.html* has a large list of IANA-reserved addresses that you can configure into your antispoofing filters.

Egress

Egress filtering prevents your network from sending spoofed packets out to the Internet. This type of filtering is desirable because it prevents your network and routers from being launching points for attacks involving spoofed packets. Not allowing spoofed packets out of your network makes your network and routers less attractive to attackers since they can no longer use spoofing attacks.

Using the same 130.18.0.0/16 network as before, to perform egress filtering, you must:

1. Create an ACL that:
   a. Allows packets with a 130.18.x.x source address out
   b. Denies all other packets
2. Apply the ACL, in the outbound direction, to the interface that connects to an external network.

For example:

```
Router#config terminal
Enter configuration commands, one per line.  End with CNTL/Z.
Router(config)#access-list 16 permit 130.18.0.0 0.0.255.255
Router(config)#access-list 16 deny any
Router(config)#interface Serial 0/0
Router(config-if)#ip access-group 16 out
Router(config-if)#^Z
```

With multiple internal networks, add permit statements for each network before the *deny any* statement. An example ACL would look like:

```
access-list 16 permit 203.2.4.0 0.0.0.255
access-list 16 permit 199.10.4.0 0.0.0.31
access-list 16 permit 215.6.45.0 0.0.0.255
access-list 16 deny any
```

 Chapter 11 is entirely about logging, but remember that you should use the *log* keyword at the end of each deny statement in your ACLs. For example, *access-list 16 deny any* becomes *access-list 16 deny any log*. The *log* keyword causes the ACL to log all violations, giving you a list of all instances when either a misconfiguration or an attacker attempted to send invalid packets through your router. See Chapter 11 for more details.

Unicast Reverse Packet Forwarding

Unicast Reverse Packet Forwarding (uRPF) is a feature designed by Cisco to make administering antispoofing on routers easier. This feature takes advantage of Cisco Express Forwarding (CEF) to make sure packets entering an interface pass a sanity check. uRPF checks the source address of each incoming packet and, based on routing information, determines if the packet should have come in on that interface. If not, the packet is discarded.

The beauty of uRPF is that it adjusts to routing and topology changes automatically. You simply enable it on an interface, and it is automatic. This means no more manual configuration and maintenance of ACLs.

uRPF does have a downside. It can have problems with asymmetrical routing. Depending on the configuration, asymmetrical routing presents the possibility of the CEF table not having enough information and discarding packets incorrectly. Because of this possibility, it is recommended that you do not enable uRPF on internal routers, but only on the edge of your network on interfaces connecting to an external network. Additionally, uRPF doesn't allow you the logging capability permitted by ACLs. uRPF logs only the number of violations, while ACLs allow you to log details about the spoofed packet.

To enable uRPF, you must first globally enable CEF with the *ip cef* command and then uRPF on each needed interface with the *ip verify unicast reverse-path* command:

```
Router#config terminal
Enter configuration commands, one per line.  End with CNTL/Z.
Router(config)#ip cef
Router(config)#interface Serial 0/1
Router(config-if)#ip verify unicast reverse-path
Router(config-if)#^Z
```

 uRPF requires that CEF be enabled. If you disable CEF while uRPF is turned on, things will stop working.

If you cannot use uRPF on your router, then you must use ACLs to eliminate spoofing. Since ACLs have a greater impact on performance than does uRPF, the following techniques may help increase performance:

1. Create smaller ACLs. Large ACLs have a much greater impact on router performance than do small ones, so make your ACLs as small as possible.

2. Apply ACLs inbound. On Cisco routers, inbound filters are more efficient than outbound filters, so modify your ACL so you can apply it inbound.

3. Use the *pass established* keyword by putting a line similar to *access-list 150 permit tcp any any established* at the top of your ACL; TCP packets with the ACK bit will be let through immediately. In return for increased performance, this may open you up to spoofed DoS attacks, but it still prevents antispoofing for all TCP connection attempts.

4. Cisco's NetFlow can also be used to increase performance. On many routers, numbered and named ACLs have been modified to work with NetFlow.

5. Some newer combinations of router software and hardware support Turbo ACLs. ACLs longer than three entries benefit from significant speed enhancements when they are compiled as a Turbo ACL.

Routing Protocol Security

The antispoofing filters discussed previously help prevent numerous attacks on your network and also keep attackers from using spoofed packets to manipulate your network's routing. Additional measures are required to finish securing your network's routing.

Static Routing

The most secure routing configuration is static routing. With static routing, an administrator manually configures each router with all appropriate routes. Static routing gives an administrator much control over how packets are passed through a network, and since routers are configured manually, there are no routing protocols for an attacker to manipulate. However, static routing has one significant drawback—it scales horribly. When moving beyond two or three routers, manually configuring static routes on each router becomes a nightmare. Furthermore, adding a new router, or even a new network to an existing router, requires you to go back and change the configuration of every single router manually. So, despite their security advantages, static routes lose their practicality when a network has frequent route changes or grows larger than three routers.

Authentication

The largest improvement to securing your routing protocol is to use authentication. Certain routing protocols such as RIP v2, OSPF, EIGRP, and BGP support authentication. When configuring authentication, you configure a routing password on each router in your network, and routing information will only be exchanged between routers that know the password. Since standard routing protocols don't use authentication by default, they are vulnerable to an attacker manipulating them. With authentication, any routing information an attacker tries to inject into your routers will be ignored (unless the attacker has the authentication password, so make sure you keep it secure.)

Next, you will find examples for configuring authentication for the interior routing protocols RIP v2, OSPF, EIGRP, and the exterior routing protocol BGP.

RIP v2

One of the problems with RIP Version 1 was its lack of support for authentication. RIP Version 2 was designed to overcome this problem. The RIP v2 protocol standard supports plain-text authentication. Cisco's implementation of RIP v2 authentication is proprietary and uses the more secure MD5 authentication to keep keys from being sent across the network in the clear.

To use RIP v2 authentication:

1. Enable RIP v2 authentication on each interface using the *ip rip authentication key-chain* command.

2. On each interface using RIP v2, configure it to use MD5 authentication instead of plain-text with the *ip rip authentication mode md5* command.

3. Configure your authentication keys on each router:

   a. Define a key chain with the *key chain* command in global configuration mode.

   b. Identify the number of your key in this chain with the *key* command.

   c. Use the *key-string* command to define the authentication key.

In the following example, RIP v2 authentication is configured on *RouterOne* using the key *UnguessableKey*. If *RouterOne* has three interfaces that are using RIP v2—Fast Ethernet 0/0, Serial 0/0, and Serial 0/1—authentication must be enabled on each interface.

This example uses key chain number 10:

```
RouterOne#config terminal
Enter configuration commands, one per line.  End with CNTL/Z.
RouterOne(config)#interface FastEthernet 0/0
RouterOne(config-if)#ip rip authentication key-chain 10
RouterOne(config-if)#ip rip authentication mode md5
RouterOne(config-if)#exit
RouterOne(config)#interface Serial 0/0
RouterOne(config-if)#ip rip authentication key-chain 10
RouterOne(config-if)#ip rip authentication mode md5
RouterOne(config-if)#exit
RouterOne(config)#interface Serial 0/1
RouterOne(config-if)#ip rip authentication key-chain 10
RouterOne(config-if)#ip rip authentication mode md5
RouterOne(config-if)#exit
RouterOne(config)#^Z
```

Next, the key chain 10 is defined. Inside key chain 10, key number 1 is created with the key-string *UnguessableKey*:

```
RouterOne#config terminal
Enter configuration commands, one per line.  End with CNTL/Z.
RouterOne(config)#key chain 10
RouterOne(config-keychain)#key 1
RouterOne(config-keychain-ke)#key-string UnguessableKey
RouterOne(config-keychain-ke)#^Z
```

Next, perform the same configuration on all of your routers. The most common misconfigurations when using authentication are:

- Not configuring RIP v2 authentication on every interface
- Not using the same key string on each router

Check these two items first if you are having trouble with RIP v2 authentication.

EIGRP

Configuring Cisco's routing protocol EIGRP to use authentication follows similar steps as configuring RIP v2 authentication:

1. Enable EIGRP authentication on each interface with the *ip authentication mode eigrp* command.

2. Define the key chain to use under each interface with the *ip authentication key-chain eigrp* command.

3. Create the key chain specified in the previous step:

    a. Define a key chain with the *key chain* command.

    b. Identify the number of this authentication key with the *key* command.

    c. Configure the actual authentication key with the *key-string* command.

Assuming your autonomous system number is 10, you would enable EIGRP authentication on the interfaced FastEthernet 0/0, Serial 0/0, and Serial 0/1 with:

```
RouterOne#config terminal
Enter configuration commands, one per line.  End with CNTL/Z.
RouterOne(config)#interface FastEthernet 0/0
RouterOne(config-if)#ip authentication mode eigrp 10 md5
RouterOne(config-if)#ip authentication key-chain eigrp 10 Chain1
RouterOne(config-if)#exit
RouterOne(config)#interface Serial 0/0
RouterOne(config-if)#ip authentication mode eigrp 10 md5
RouterOne(config-if)#ip authentication key-chain eigrp 10 Chain1
RouterOne(config-if)#exit
RouterOne(config)#interface Serial 0/1
RouterOne(config-if)#ip authentication mode eigrp 10 md5
RouterOne(config-if)#ip authentication key-chain eigrp 10 Chain1
RouterOne(config-if)#exit
RouterOne(config)#^Z
```

After your interfaces are configured to use EIGRP authentication, you then define the key chain and the authentication key. The previous commands specify *Chain1* as the key chain to use for authentication, so the *key chain* command needs to be used to create *Chain1*. In the following example, the authentication key *1* is defined as *UnguessableKey*:

```
RouterOne#config terminal
Enter configuration commands, one per line.  End with CNTL/Z.
RouterOne(config)#key chain Chain1
RouterOne(config-keychain)#key 1
RouterOne(config-keychain-ke)#key-string UnguessageKey
RouterOne(config-keychain-ke)#^Z
```

Perform this same configuration on all other routers and interfaces that require EIGRP authentication to complete the setup.

OSPF

Configuring OSPF authentication is a little simpler than with RIP v2. Like RIP, OSPF can use both plain-text and MD5 authentication. These examples only cover using secure MD5 authentication. If you are using OSPF as your interior routing protocol to configure authentication:

1. Use the *ip ospf message-digest-key* command on each interface to define a key. This includes defining both the key number and the actual authentication key itself.

2. Use the *area ? authentication message-digest* command to configure OSPF to use authentication.

Using the interfaces as in the RIP v2 example, configure OSPF authentication on interfaced FastEthernet 0/0, Serial 0/0, and Serial 0/1:

```
RouterOne#config terminal
Enter configuration commands, one per line.  End with CNTL/Z.
RouterOne(config)#interface FastEthernet 0/0
RouterOne(config-if)#ip ospf message-digest-key 1 md5 UnguessableKey
RouterOne(config-if)#exit
RouterOne(config)#interface Serial 0/0
RouterOne(config-if)#ip ospf message-digest-key 1 md5 UnguessableKey
RouterOne(config-if)#exit
RouterOne(config)#interface Serial 0/1
RouterOne(config-if)#ip ospf message-digest-key 1 md5 UnguessableKey
RouterOne(config-if)#exit
RouterOne(config)#^Z
```

Next, configure authentication under the OSPF areas where you want to use authentication. This example assumes that your OSPF autonomous number is 10 and that you are setting up area 0 to use authentication:

```
RouterOne#config terminal
Enter configuration commands, one per line.  End with CNTL/Z.
RouterOne(config)#router ospf 10
RouterOne(config-router)#area 0 authentication message-digest
RouterOne(config-router)#^Z
```

Repeat these steps on your other routers and their interfaces using OSPF authentication to complete the setup.

 It is important to note that if authentication is enabled on one OSPF link, then it must be enabled on all other links within that area, or OSPF adjacency can be lost.

BGP

BGP authentication is one of the simplest to configure. BGP doesn't support plain-text authentication, only MD5, so there is no need to explicitly specify MD5 authentication. Enable BGP authentication by adding the password keyword to the *neighbor* command. For example, your router's BGP autonomous number is 109, and 130.18.6.7 is configured as a BGP neighbor; you can enable authentication between *RouterOne* and 130.18.6.7 with:

```
RouterOne#config terminal
Enter configuration commands, one per line.  End with CNTL/Z.
RouterOne(config)#router bgp 109
RouterOne(config-router)#neighbor 130.18.6.7 password MyBGPpassword
RouterOne(config-router)#^Z
```

Next, use the same commands to configure 130.18.6.7 to authenticate with *Router-One*. The only difference is that you use *RouterOne's* IP address instead of 130.18.6.7. Assuming *RouterOne* has the IP 19.6.7.8, this would look like:

```
RouterTwo#config terminal
Enter configuration commands, one per line.  End with CNTL/Z.
RouterTwo(config)#router bgp 109
RouterTwo(config-router)#neighbor 19.6.7.8 password MyBGPpassword
RouterTwo(config-router)#^Z
```

Repeat this configuration with each neighbor you want to use BGP authentication.

Passive Interfaces

Sometimes you want to control the routing information that is sent out or accepted into an interface. This can be done with passive interfaces and route filtering. Using passive interfaces is the easiest way to keep an interface from participating in exchanging routing protocols, but passive interfaces are an all-or-nothing approach. Route filtering can be used when you need an interface to send and receive only specific routing information.

Passive interfaces

When an interface is configured as a passive interface, it stops sending out routing updates. Passive interfaces with most routing protocols—OSPF and EIGRP being the notable exceptions—will still receive routing updates. Passive interfaces are often used on network segments that require the security of static routes or when routing updates should not be sent out for both bandwidth and security reasons.

To configure an interface as a passive interface, from global configuration mode, enter your routing protocol mode with commands such as *router rip* or router *ospf 109*. Next, use the *passive-interface* command followed by the interface you want to stop sending out updates. For example, using RIP, if you wanted to make interface FastEthernet 0/2 a passive interface:

```
RouterOne#config terminal
Enter configuration commands, one per line.  End with CNTL/Z.
RouterOne(config)#router rip
RouterOne(config-router)#passive-interface FastEthernet 0/2
RouterOne(config-router)#^Z
```

The *passive-interface* command would be repeated for every interface you wanted to configure as passive.

OSPF and EIGRP passive interfaces

Unlike passive interfaces in most other protocols, passive interfaces in EIGRP and OSPF not only stop sending routing updates, but also stop receiving them. To have an interface under these protocols stop sending, but still receive routing updates, you must enable EIGRP or OSPF on the interface and then use an outbound routing filter to prevent the sending out of routing updates.

Route Filtering

Route filtering gives you more control over what routing information is sent or received on an interface. Use the *distribute-list <ACL> out* command to control outbound routing information and *distribute-list <ACL> in* to control inbound information. These filters are configured under the router's routing protocol configuration mode and can be configured to apply globally to the entire router or to an individual interface.

Global filtering

To configure route filtering globally:

1. Create an ACL that defines what network information is allowed in/out.

2. Configure a *distribute-list* in the appropriate direction under the router's routing protocol configuration.

For example, if *RouterOne* uses EIGRP (AS number 110) and you do not want it to send out routing information about network 130.18.0.0/16, configure an outbound filter with the *distribute-list <ACL> out* command:

```
RouterOne#config terminal
Enter configuration commands, one per line.  End with CNTL/Z.
RouterOne(config)#access-list 14 deny 130.18.0.0 0.0.255.255
RouterOne(config)#access-list 14 permit any
RouterOne(config)#router eigrp 110
RouterOne(config-router)#distribute-list 14 out
RouterOne(config-router)#^Z
```

Using the same example, but configuring *RouterOne* to ignore any routing information it receives about network 130.18.0.0/16, use the *distribute-list <ACL> in* command:

```
RouterOne#config terminal
Enter configuration commands, one per line.  End with CNTL/Z.
RouterOne(config)#access-list 14 deny 130.18.0.0 0.0.255.255
RouterOne(config)#access-list 14 permit any
RouterOne(config)#router eigrp 110
RouterOne(config-router)#distribute-list 14 in
RouterOne(config-router)#^Z
```

Per-interface filtering

To apply filtering to a specific interface, add the name of the interface after the *distribute-list* command. For example, to keep only interface Serial 0/0 from sending out routing information about network 130.18.0.0/16, refer to this example:

```
RouterOne#config terminal
Enter configuration commands, one per line.  End with CNTL/Z.
RouterOne(config)#access-list 14 deny 130.18.0.0 0.0.255.255
RouterOne(config)#access-list 14 permit any
RouterOne(config)#router eigrp 110
RouterOne(config-router)#distribute-list 14 out Serial 0/0
RouterOne(config-router)#^Z
```

Notice that the only line that has changed from our previous example was the line *distribute-list 14 out Serial 0/0*, in which *Serial 0/0* was appended to indicate that this filter applies only to routing updates sent out of Serial 0/0.

In addition to distribute lists, BGP allows you to filter routes by neighbor and use prefix lists that have advantages over ACLs. See Cisco's documentation on BGP for more details on how to use these methods of route filtering.

Filtering at network borders

Route filtering is generally used between external and internal networks. Route filtering at the borders of your network helps minimize the chance that incorrect routing information will be injected into your network without requiring the administrative hassle of creating and maintaining filters on every interface on your network. For example, if network 14.6.0.0/16 is controlled by one of your customers, and you receive routing information for this network from routers controlled by that customer, good security dictates that you configure your border routers to accept only routing updates about the 14.6.0.0/16 network from the customer. This prevents misconfigurations or attackers on the customer's network from sending false routing information to your routers.

Routing Protocol and Antispoofing Checklist

This checklist summarizes the important security information presented in this chapter. A complete security checklist is provided in Appendix A.

- Take antispoofing measures at each router bordering an external network:
  - Enable *ip verify unicast reverse-path* on all interfaces that connect with external networks and are not involved in asymmetrical routing.
  - If uRPF cannot be used (or additional logging is required), apply antispoofing ingress and egress ACLs to all interfaces that connect to an external network.
  - If your network is very small and you need additional security, consider using static routes.

- When using a routing protocol, choose one that supports authentication and enable authentication on all routers on the network:
  - Choose the authentication password well and make sure controls are in place to keep the authentication passwords secret.
  - Use secure hash protocols such as MD5, not plain-text protocols, for authentication.
- Use route filters at the border between your network and the networks controlled by others to prevent false routing information from being injected into your network.

CHAPTER 10

NTP

Time is inherently important to the function of routers and networks. It provides the only frame of reference between all devices on the network. This makes synchronized time extremely important. Without synchronized time, accurately correlating information between devices becomes difficult, if not impossible. When it comes to security, if you cannot successfully compare logs between each of your routers and all your network servers, you will find it very hard to develop a reliable picture of an incident. Finally, even if you are able to put the pieces together, unsynchronized times, especially between log files, may give an attacker with a good attorney enough wiggle room to escape prosecution.

NTP Overview

The Network Time Protocol (NTP) was first described in RFC 958 and has developed into the standard Internet time synchronization protocol. It is extremely efficient and needs no more than about one packet a minute to synchronize systems on a LAN to within 1 millisecond, and systems across WANs to within about 10 milliseconds.

Without proper time synchronization between your routers, you may not only have trouble with correlating log files, but inaccurate time may also affect your ability to perform accounting, fault analysis, network management, and even time-based AAA authentication and authorization. So good time management is a necessary part of keeping your network healthy and secure.

 While NTP Version 4 is the latest and preferred version of NTP, Cisco routers currently only support through Version 3.

NTP can operate in four different modes—client, server, peer, and broadcast. These modes provide NTP with a great amount of flexibility in how you configure synchronization on your network.

NTP modes differ based on how NTP allows communication between systems. NTP communication consists of time requests and control queries. Time requests provide the standard client/server relationship in which a client requests time synchronization from an NTP server. Control queries provide ways for remote systems to get configuration information and reconfigure NTP servers. Here is a short explanation of the NTP modes:

Client

> An NTP client is configured to let its clock be set and synchronized by an external NTP timeserver. NTP clients can be configured to use multiple servers to set their local time and are able to give preference to the most accurate time sources. They will not, however, provide synchronization services to any other devices.

Server

> An NTP server is configured to synchronize NTP clients. Servers can be configured to synchronize any client or only specific clients. NTP servers, however, will accept no synchronization information from their clients and therefore will not let clients update or affect the server's time settings.

Peer

> With NTP peers, one NTP-enabled device does not have authority over the other. With the peering model, each device shares its time information with the other, and each device can also provide time synchronization to the other.

Broadcast/multicast

> Broadcast/multicast mode is a special server mode with which the NTP server broadcasts its synchronization information to all clients. Broadcast mode requires that clients be on the same subnet as the server, and multicast mode requires that clients and servers have multicast access available and configured.

Configuring NTP

The three most common configurations for NTP are the use of a central server, a hierarchical model, or a flat configuration. Each of these configurations has advantages and disadvantages, discussed next.

Central Server

The central server configuration is probably the easiest for small- to medium-sized networks. With this configuration, you set up one or two centralized NTP servers that use the Internet (or other authoritative source) to synchronize their time. All clients on the network are then configured to synchronize their time to those servers. This type of configuration is easy to administer and simplifies authorization and access control. However, because it relies on a few central servers, it doesn't scale as well as the hierarchical model on larger networks.

NTP Accuracy and Reliability

For maximum time reliability, you can set up what is called a *stratum one server*, an NTP server directly connected to radio receivers or atomic clocks that are extremely accurate. An NTP stratum two server is one that gets its time information from a stratum one server, and so on. You can synchronize your systems on the Internet to several stratum two and three servers. Some of these servers are free, and others offer slightly greater accuracy and reliability at a cost.

NTP experts recommend that for the greatest reliability and accuracy, you need a minimum of three internal NTP servers with each server synchronized with three different external NTP servers. These internal servers are then set up to peer one another in case one of the servers loses contact with its external NTP servers. Internal NTP clients are then configured to synchronize with all three of the internal NTP servers. The recommendations extend further to putting each NTP server in different buildings and providing different paths to the Internet for each server.

For many smaller networks, the cost of such reliability is difficult to justify, and in the absence of other mitigating factors, many smaller networks run NTP successfully with one or two NTP servers synchronized through a single Internet connection.

 There are several publicly accessible NTP timeservers on the Internet. Do a search on the Internet for public NTP servers or see *http://www. eecis.udel.edu/~mills/ntp/servers.htm*.

Existing timeserver

If you already have an existing NTP server set up on your network, it is relatively easy to configure your routers to use that server for time synchronization. The command *ntp server*, followed by the IP address or hostname of the NTP server, is used to configure your router to use an existing NTP server:

```
Router#config terminal
Enter configuration commands, one per line.  End with CNTL/Z.
Router(config)#ntp server 129.237.32.2
Router(config)#^Z
```

To specify additional timeservers for redundancy, simply repeat the *ntp server* command with the IP address of each additional server.

 If your router has an internal clock chip, once you have NTP configured, you can use it to synchronize the time of the internal clock with the *ntp update-calendar* command.

Synchronized router as a timeserver

Once a router is synchronized with another time source, either as a client or a peer, that router will automatically provide time synchronization for other systems. This allows you to use one or more routers as the primary time synchronization sources for your LAN. To do this:

1. Pick one, two, or three routers and have them synchronize to separate external time sources.

2. Configure your internal servers and systems to use these routers for their time synchronization.

 Some low-end routers, such as the 1600 and 1700 series, don't support the full NTP protocol. They support only a stripped-down version called *SNTP*. SNTP is a client-only version of NTP and can be configured with the *sntp server* command.

Unsynchronized router as a timeserver

If you do not have an existing timeserver, you should synchronize your routers to public NTP servers on the Internet and use them as timeservers for your internal network. In situations in which this is not possible, such as isolated networks, you can configure an unsynchronized router to act as an authoritative NTP source using the *ntp master* command. Cisco and NTP experts discourage the use of this command if any other NTP time sources are available because it violates NTP's hierarchical trust model. When using this command, you should choose a high stratum number, such as 10, so time associations through the fake master clock are ignored if more trustworthy NTP information is made available.

To enable an unsynchronized Cisco router to act as an authoritative NTP clock at stratum 10, type:

```
Router#config terminal
Enter configuration commands, one per line.  End with CNTL/Z.
Router(config)#ntp master 10
Router(config)#^Z
```

Again, once a router's clock is synchronized to an NTP source or configured to serve as a master, it will, in turn, act as an NTP server to any system that requests synchronization. It is important to use authentication and access lists to avoid providing time synchronization service to the entire Internet.

Flat

The flat structure configures all routers to peer with one another; each router acts as both a client and a server with every other router. Then two or three routers that are geographically separated are configured to point to external timeservers.

The primary advantage of this model is that it is very stable; each router has the ability to provide synchronizing information to every other router. The disadvantages are lack of scalability, difficulty of administration, and a slow time to convergence. When you configure a full mesh in which every router peers with every other router, all routers have a say in the final time synchronization. Therefore, it takes longer to get all the routers to agree on the exact time. On larger networks, the most serious disadvantages are the lack of scalability and difficulty of administration. Whenever you add a router to the mesh, you must reconfigure every router on that mesh to peer with the new router.

If you have a smaller network and choose to use the flat model, use the *ntp peer* command to configure each router to peer with all other routers. If your network consists of five routers—*RouterOne* through *RouterFive*—to configure an NTP mesh, the commands on *RouterOne* would be:

```
Router#config terminal
Enter configuration commands, one per line.  End with CNTL/Z.
Router(config)#ntp peer RouterTwo
Router(config)#ntp peer RouterThree
Router(config)#ntp peer RouterFour
Router(config)#ntp peer RouterFive
Router(config)#^Z
```

To complete the flat NTP mesh, each router must be configured with similar commands, peering it with all other routers on the network. Finally, to synchronize the mesh with external NTP servers, you would pick two or three geographically separated routers and use the *ntp server* command to synchronize them to the external timeservers.

Hierarchical

For larger networks, the hierarchical model is probably the most scalable and easiest to administer. This model is typically used by ISPs that have multiple stratum one servers that synchronize all internal ISP systems and routers. These routers, in turn, provide time synchronization for customer routers. The customer routers then provide time synchronization to the customer's internal systems. With this tree-like model, both administration and time to convergence is minimized.

If the top of your NTP network consisted of *RouterOne*, *RouterTwo*, and *RouterThree*, you would synchronize these routers to external servers. For example, using external timeservers 129.237.32.2, 128.249.2.2, and 128.118.25.3 would each be configured with:

```
Router#config terminal
Enter configuration commands, one per line.  End with CNTL/Z.
Router(config)#ntp server 129.237.32.2
Router(config)#ntp server 128.249.2.2
Router(config)#ntp server 128.118.25.3
Router(config)#^Z
```

Next, each of these three routers would be configured to peer with the others. This would provide consistent and accurate time, even if a router lost connectivity to the Internet. *RouterOne* would be configured to peer with *RouterTwo* and *RouterThree* with the following commands:

```
Router#config terminal
Enter configuration commands, one per line.  End with CNTL/Z.
Router(config)#ntp peer RouterTwo
Router(config)#ntp peer RouterThree
Router(config)#^Z
```

Next, each customer's gateway router would be configured to use the internal ISP routers for NTP synchronization:

```
Router#config terminal
Enter configuration commands, one per line.  End with CNTL/Z.
Router(config)#ntp server RouterOne
Router(config)#ntp server RouterTwo
Router(config)#ntp server RouterThree
Router(config)#^Z
```

Finally, the customer's internal systems and routers would be configured to use the customer's gateway router for time synchronization.

NTP Options

NTP on Cisco routers support additional options that may be useful for synchronization, keeping the router from being overwhelmed by NTP requests, and disabling NTP on only specific interfaces.

Preferred server

A router can be configured to prefer an NTP source over another. A preferred server's responses are discarded only if they vary dramatically from the other time sources. Otherwise, the preferred server is used for synchronization without consideration of the other time sources. Preferred servers are usually specified when they are known to be extremely accurate. To specify a preferred server, use the *prefer* keyword appended to the *ntp server* command. The following example tells the router to prefer *TimeServerOne* over *TimeServerTwo*:

```
Router#config terminal
Enter configuration commands, one per line.  End with CNTL/Z.
Router(config)#ntp server TimeServerOne prefer
Router(config)#ntp server TimeServerTwo
Router(config)#^Z
```

ntp max-associations

NTP also allows you to define the maximum number of peer and client associations that your router will serve. This helps ensure that your router isn't overwhelmed by huge numbers of NTP synchronization requests. The *ntp max-associations* command is used to set this limit. For example:

```
RouterOne#config terminal
Enter configuration commands, one per line.  End with CNTL/Z.
RouterOne(config)#ntp max-associations 20
RouterOne(config)#^Z
```

ntp disable

The *ntp disable* command can be used on a per-interface basis. When applied to an interface, the command keeps the interface from acting as an NTP server, but still allows it to serve as an NTP client. This is the recommended configuration for external interfaces. If Serial 0/0 is the external interface, you can keep it from acting as an NTP server with:

```
RouterOne#config terminal
Enter configuration commands, one per line.  End with CNTL/Z.
RouterOne(config)#interface serial 0/0
RouterOne(config-if)#ntp disable
RouterOne(config-if)#^Z
```

Time Zones

NTP uses Coordinated Universal Time for all time synchronizations so it is not affected by different time zones. To have your router report the time in your local time zone, you need to use the *clock timezone* and *clock summer-time* commands. The clock *timezone* command needs to be followed by the time zone abbreviation and the time zone offset. For example, to set your routers' local time zone to eastern standard time, enter:

```
Router#config terminal
Enter configuration commands, one per line.  End with CNTL/Z.
Router(config)#clock timezone EST -05
Router(config)#^Z
```

To enable daylight saving time, the *clock summer-time* command requires the daylight savings time abbreviation of your time zone followed by the keyword *recurring*. Configuring eastern daylight time would require:

```
Router#config terminal
Enter configuration commands, one per line.  End with CNTL/Z.
Router(config)#clock summer-time EDT recurring
Router(config)#^Z
```

Cisco routers are configured to U.S. time zone standards. If you are in a location with different time standards, you can still use the *clock timezone* and the *clock summer-time* commands to customize the time zone and daylight saving time settings. Refer to Cisco documentation for more details.

Viewing Status

To verify that your router is synchronizing correctly, use the *show ntp* command. First, the *show ntp status* command tells you that you are synchronized, the stratum level of your router, and the IP of the server to which you are synchronized. For example, a *show ntp status* on a system synchronized to 128.249.2.2 shows:

```
Router#show ntp status
Clock is synchronized, stratum 3, reference is 128.249.2.2
nominal freq is 250.0000 Hz, actual freq is 249.9961 Hz, precision is 2**16
reference time is BF454660.7CCA9683 (22:37:36.487 EDT Sat Sep 8 2001)
clock offset is 4.3323 msec, root delay is 136.28 msec
root dispersion is 37.69 msec, peer dispersion is 1.14 msec
```

The first line shows the system to which the router is synchronized and that it is acting as a stratum 3 NTP server.

Next, the *show ntp associations* command lists all the NTP servers to which the router is configured to synchronize. An example *show ntp associations* would display:

```
Router#show ntp associations

       address         ref clock     st  when  poll reach  delay  offset    disp
  *~128.249.2.2       192.5.41.40     2    4    64   377    76.9    5.49     0.4
  -~130.218.100.5     198.72.72.10    3    33   128  377     7.1   13.13     0.6
  +~129.237.32.2      192.43.244.18   2    16   64   377    44.8    3.05     0.9
  +~128.118.25.3      128.118.25.12   2    48   64   377    39.7    5.50     1.4
   * master (synced), # master (unsynced), + selected, - candidate, ~ configured
```

The asterisk (*) next to the 128.249.2.2 address indicates that the router is synchronized to this server. It is very important that at least one address have an asterisk by it. NTP dictates that a server cannot synchronize another system unless the server itself is synchronized.

 After configuring a router to act as an NTP server, it may take five to ten minutes before that router becomes synchronized with other time sources. Until the router is synchronized, it does not provide time synchronization for other systems. This is important to remember so you can avoid troubleshooting problems that don't exist. After you configure a router as an NTP server, you may need to wait a few minutes before it successfully provides synchronization for other systems.

Access Lists

Once a router is synchronized to an NTP time source, it automatically acts as an NTP for any client that requests synchronization or informational control queries. Many network administrators leave their routers open to NTP requests from the Internet. The problem with this is that Murphy (of Murphy's law) guarantees that the day you say "There is no harm in letting people get time information off the routers, so I won't bother restricting access" is the same day a new security vulnerability in NTP will be discovered. Also, if your routers get listed as public timeservers on the Web, you can get overwhelmed with public time synchronization requests. Finally, with a sophisticated attack, an attacker could use NTP informational queries to discover the timeservers to which your router is synchronized, and then through an attack such as DNS cache poisoning, redirect your router to a system under his control. Manipulating the time on your routers this way could make it difficult to identify when incidents truly happened and could also be used to confuse any time-based security measures you have in place.

NTP allows you to configure ACLs to restrict access to the NTP services on the router. These ACLs can be configured to restrict access based on IP and the following four restrictions:

peer
> Allows time synchronization requests and control queries and allows the router to synchronize itself to remote systems that pass the ACL

serve
> Allows time synchronization requests and control queries, but does not allow the router to synchronize itself to remote systems that pass the ACL

serve-only
> Allows only time synchronization requests from systems that pass the ACL

query-only
> Allows only NTP control queries from systems that pass the ACL

The two ACLs generally used to restrict access for security reasons are the *peer* and *serve-only* options—for example, if you are using the hierarchical model with the core routers *RouterOne* and *RouterTwo* providing NTP services for the rest of the routers in your network.

First, configure *RouterOne*:

1. To use three external NTP servers with the *ntp server* command.
2. To peer with *RouterTwo* with the *ntp peer* command.
3. To peer only with *RouterTwo*. Assuming *RouterTwo*'s IP is 135.26.2.1, you:
   a. Configure an ACL to restrict access only to *RouterTwo*.
   b. Configure NTP to use the ACL with the *ntp access-group peer* command.
4. To provide time services only to internal systems. For this example, assume your internal network is 135.26.x.x.
   a. Configure an ACL to restrict access to internal systems:
   b. Configure NTP to use the ACL with the *ntp access-group serve-only* command:

```
RouterOne#config terminal
Enter configuration commands, one per line.  End with CNTL/Z.
RouterOne(config)#ntp server 128.250.36.2
RouterOne(config)#ntp server 140.79.17.101
```

```
RouterOne(config)#ntp server 138.194.21.154
RouterOne(config)#ntp peer RouterTwo
RouterOne(config)#access-list 20 permit 135.26.2.1 0.0.0.0
RouterOne(config)#access-list 20 deny any
RouterOne(config)#ntp access-group peer 20
RouterOne(config)#access-list 21 permit 135.26.0.0 0.0.255.255
RouterOne(config)#access-list 21 deny any
RouterOne(config)#ntp access-group serve-only 21
RouterOne(config)#^Z
```

RouterTwo would be configured the same way with references to *RouterTwo* replaced by *RouterOne*. For optimal redundancy, you should have *RouterTwo* configured to use different public NTP servers than *RouterOne*.

NTP Source Address

On a router with multiple interfaces, the source address of the NTP packet is the same as the interface the packet it sent out on. This arrangement can complicate things when you are trying to create simple ACLs and use authentication. To make administration easier, use the *ntp source* command.

For example, if your Fast Ethernet 0/0 interface has the IP address 135.26.100.1 and you want all NTP packets from this router to use this as their source address, type:

```
RouterOne#config terminal
Enter configuration commands, one per line.  End with CNTL/Z.
RouterOne(config)#ntp source FastEthernet0/0
RouterOne(config)#^Z
```

Now you can configure all of your ACLs to allow or deny access based on the 135.26.100.1 IP address.

 Many administrators choose to use the loopback interface as the source. The loopback never fails and therefore isn't affected if another interface goes down.

Authentication

For additional security, you can configure your NTP servers and clients to use authentication. Cisco routers support only MD5 authentication for NTP. To enable a router to do NTP authentication:

1. Enable NTP authentication with the *ntp authenticate* command.
2. Define an NTP authentication key with the *ntp authentication-key* command. A unique number identifies each NTP key. This number is the first argument to the *ntp authentication-key* command.
3. Use the *ntp trusted-key* command to tell the router which keys are valid for authentication. The *ntp trusted-key* command's only argument is the number of the key defined in the previous step.

To enable authentication on *RouterOne* and define key number 10 as *MySecretKey*, type:

```
RouterOne#config terminal
Enter configuration commands, one per line.  End with CNTL/Z.
RouterOne(config)#ntp authenticate
RouterOne(config)#ntp authentication-key 10 md5 MySecretKey
RouterOne(config)#ntp trusted-key 10
RouterOne(config)#^Z
```

 Configuring NTP authentication does not require all clients to use NTP authentication; it enables clients to use authentication. Your router will still respond to unauthenticated requests, so be sure to use ACLs to limit NTP access.

If your external NTP servers require authentication, you need to configure your router to use authentication when contacting those servers. To do this, perform the same steps listed previously to add an NTP authentication key; then use the *ntp server* command with the key argument to tell the router what key to use when authenticating with the NTP server:

```
RouterOne#config terminal
Enter configuration commands, one per line.  End with CNTL/Z.
RouterOne(config)#ntp authenticate
RouterOne(config)#ntp authentication-key 11 md5 MyOtherKey
RouterOne(config)#ntp trusted-key 11
RouterOne(config)#ntp server 130.218.59.4 key 11
RouterOne(config)#^Z
```

Finally, to authenticate NTP peers, configure the same key on both systems and use the *ntp peer* command with the key argument to configure authentication:

```
RouterOne#config terminal
Enter configuration commands, one per line.  End with CNTL/Z.
RouterOne(config)#ntp authenticate
RouterOne(config)#ntp authentication-key 12 md5 MyPeeringKey
RouterOne(config)#ntp trusted-key 12
RouterOne(config)#ntp peer 135.26.100.2 key 12
RouterOne(config)#^Z
```

NTP Checklist

This checklist summarizes the important security information presented in this chapter. A complete security checklist is provided in Appendix A.

- Make sure all routers use NTP to synchronize their time.
- On larger networks requiring more accurate time, use redundant timeservers and synchronize routers to multiple servers to prevent a single point of failure.

- Use the *ntp master* command only when external time synchronization is not possible—i.e., in networks not connected to the Internet.
- Make sure all routers have ACLs preventing them from becoming public time synchronization servers. These ACLs should restrict what servers the router synchronizes to and systems the router will synchronize.
- Use NTP authentication between clients, servers, and peers to ensure that time is synchronized to approved servers only.

CHAPTER 11
Logging

Good logging is important for real-time incident detection and after-the-fact auditing. By religiously watching your log file, you will often get warnings that an outage is about to occur or that an attacker is analyzing your network for vulnerabilities. This allows you to take action to correct or prevent the problem. Log files also provide an audit trail for determining what went wrong or what an attacker accomplished.

Logging in General

Logging is a balance between collecting as much useful information as possible and not collecting so much information that it overwhelms you. An administrator overwhelmed by log files will ignore them until after an incident occurs. This negates the first benefit of log files—early warning. Many network administrators keep the default logging setting on routers and never take advantage of all of the additional information that can be logged. The rest of this chapter covers the logging capabilities of Cisco routers and discusses how to avoid being overwhelmed by your log files.

To achieve maximum benefit from log files, you must monitor them regularly. On systems of medium importance, log review can be done daily with the results emailed to the administrator. On highly secure systems, log analysis is often done in real time with the results sent to a pager.

Numerous commercial and public domain software packages can help you analyze your log files. Use them. These packages automate the process of analyzing log files by filtering out uninteresting messages and highlighting the dangerous ones. Such programs are the only way an administrator can keep up with log files to use them for incident detection.

One of the most useful ways to set up your log-watching programs is to have them:

1. Highlight everything you know is dangerous.
2. Ignore everything you know is safe.
3. Print out everything else.

Before you run the log checker the first time, go through your current logs and configure the software to highlight or ignore each different entry. Each day, run the log-check software, taking note of any highlighted (dangerous) messages. Next, for each message the software didn't highlight or ignore, configure the software to do one or the other. After about two weeks of doing this daily, you will have a custom configuration that will automatically inform you of dangerous log messages while stripping out all extraneous ones. If all your routers log to a central *syslog* server, monitoring your logs becomes even easier, since everything can be monitored from one location and you need only a single log-checking configuration.

Router Logging

Cisco routers can log information in six ways:

Console logging
> Console log messages are configured to be displayed on the console port only. You must be connected to the console port to see these messages.

Buffered logging
> Buffered logging keeps the log messages in RAM on the router. A logging buffer must be configured on the router, and this buffer is circular, meaning that when it fills up, the oldest log message is deleted to make room for the new message.

Terminal logging
> Using the *terminal monitor* command, routers can be configured to send log messages to the VTY terminals.

syslog
> Cisco routers can be configured to send their log messages to one or more external *syslog* servers.

SNMP traps
> If enabled, SNMP can be configured to send traps to an external SNMP server to log specific conditions.

AAA accounting
> If you are using AAA, you can configure the router to log network connections and even command execution to the Network Access Server (NAS).

Log messages are given a priority from 0 to 7. The lower the number, the more critical the message. These levels are defined as shown in Table 11-1.

Table 11-1. Log severity levels

Level	Title	Description
0	Emergencies	System is unusable.
1	Alerts	Immediate action is needed.
2	Critical	A critical condition has occurred.

Table 11-1. Log severity levels (continued)

Level	Title	Description
3	Errors	An error condition has occurred.
4	Warning	A warning message.
5	Notifications	Normal but significant events.
6	Informational	Information messages.
7	Debugging	Debugging messages.

These levels are a hierarchy in which messages of your chosen level and above are logged and printed. Choosing level 7 (debugging) will print out all messages from level 7 to 0, while choosing level 2 (critical) will only print out messages of levels 2 to 0.

Timestamps

The importance of accurate time was addressed in Chapter 10. It is also important to make sure that all log messages include detailed time information. Without this information, it becomes impossible to precisely correlate various log files to determine when an incident happened. To configure Cisco routers to include detailed time information in all log messages, use the *service timestamps log datetime* command. Use the following options to make sure as much information as possible is captured:

msec
> This option includes milliseconds in each log timestamp. Without this option, log messages are timestamped only to the nearest second.

localtime
> This option configures the routers to use the local time to timestamp each log message. Doing so is generally advisable to make the logs easier for a human to interpret, but may be left out when routers across different time zones are logging to a central *syslog* server.

show-timezone
> This option configures the router to indicate the time zone when timestamping each message. This step makes comparing log messages from various sources much easier.

To enable this detailed timestamping:

```
RouterOne#config terminal
Enter configuration commands, one per line.  End with CNTL/Z.
RouterOne(config)#service timestamps log datetime msec localtime show-timezone
RouterOne(config)#^Z
```

Console Logging

To see console messages, you must be logged into the console. The console is configured by default to level 5 (notifications), meaning that it only displays messages of notification level or above.

Changing the console logging level

To change the logging level of the console, use the *logging console* command, followed by the number or name of the new severity level. To see all logging messages, set the console to level 7 (debug) by:

```
RouterOne#config terminal
Enter configuration commands, one per line.  End with CNTL/Z.
RouterOne(config)#logging console 7
RouterOne(config)#^Z
```

or

```
RouterOne#config terminal
Enter configuration commands, one per line.  End with CNTL/Z.
RouterOne(config)#logging console debugging
RouterOne(config)#^Z
```

Disabling console logging

As you begin logging more information, you may have trouble using the console as the display is covered up by numerous log messages. You can eliminate some of these messages by changing to a higher severity level using the commands described or you can disable logging to the console altogether. Since each console log message requires a CPU interrupt to be delivered, disabling logging in the console port can increase a router's performance. Disabling console logging is done by:

```
RouterOne#config terminal
Enter configuration commands, one per line.  End with CNTL/Z.
RouterOne(config)#no logging console
RouterOne(config)#^Z
```

Buffered Logging

Buffered logging keeps copies of log messages in the router's RAM. This makes it very easy for an administrator logged into the router to display current log messages. The RAM buffer is circular. The buffer is a fixed size, and as new messages are added to the buffer, the older messages are deleted. This keeps the most recent messages in the buffer without filling up the router's memory.

The size of each router's logging buffer should be configured with regard to the amount of RAM on the router. These buffers should be large enough to keep useful log entries, but small enough not to use up the router's RAM and interfere with performance. A size of 16,000 or 32,000 bytes is usually sufficient and doesnt overwhelm the router. Play with the values if you find that you need log messages kept longer.

To enable buffered logging:

1. Make sure logging is turned on with the *logging on* command.

2. Configure the buffer with the *logging buffered* command.

3. Configure the logging buffer severity level with the *logging buffered* command.

The following example configures the router to use a 32,000-byte logging buffer and to log messages of level 6 (informational) and above:

```
RouterOne#config terminal
Enter configuration commands, one per line.  End with CNTL/Z.
RouterOne(config)#logging on
RouterOne(config)#logging buffered 32000
RouterOne(config)#logging buffered informational
RouterOne(config)#^Z
```

Terminal Monitor

While logging is enabled to the console by default, log messages are not normally sent to the VTYs. If you are logged in through the network on a VTY and want to see log messages on your terminal, use the *terminal monitor* command:

1. Use the *logging monitor* command to configure the severity of messages sent to the VTY terminal.

2. At the enable prompt of the terminal, type **terminal monitor**.

The following example configures the terminal to receive level 3 (error) messages and above:

```
RouterOne#config terminal
Enter configuration commands, one per line.  End with CNTL/Z.
RouterOne(config)#logging monitor error
RouterOne(config)#^Z
RouterOne#terminal monitor
```

Note that the *terminal monitor* command was run not from configuration mode, but rather from privileged or enable mode.

Turning on *terminal monitor*, especially at the debug level, can overwhelm your connection, so be careful. If you find your terminal session scrolling with so many log messages that you are overwhelmed, use the *terminal no monitor* command to stop the terminal from receiving the log messages. Even if you can't see what you are typing, try typing **terminal no monitor** and pressing Enter; the router will still take the command and stop the log messages to your terminal.

syslog

syslog logging is the most important non-AAA method of logging. All previous logging methods print the log message to a terminal or keep the log in memory. Neither of these records the log messages long term. Long-term storage is critical for keeping audit trails and is required for analyzing logs after messages have left the terminal screen or have buffered out of memory.

Almost all Unix servers come with *syslog* servers configured by default. Almost all security-conscious organization have one or two central *syslog* servers in which all logging information is sent and recorded. These messages are sent across the network to the *syslog* server where the server records the message to the hard drive. Centralizing your log files in this method makes correlating log information from different routers and systems much easier.

Remember to configure your router to send all log messages to a *syslog* server so that messages are permanently recorded and not lost when the router runs out of memory or messages scroll off the terminal screen.

syslog facilities

syslog servers rely on the severity levels defined earlier and on another variable called the *facility*. *syslog* facilities separate different services so that log messages can be separated into different log files. This separation makes reviewing and auditing log files much easier. Table 11-2 lists some standard *syslog* facilities.

Table 11-2. syslog facilities

syslog facility	Description
User	Log messages generated by user processes
Kern	Log messages generated by the kernel
Mail	Log messages regarding the mail system
Daemon	Log messages generated by system daemons
Auth	Log messages regarding the authorization system
LPR	Log messages regarding the printing system
News	Log messages regarding Usenet news processes
UUCP	Reserved for the UUCP system
Cron	Log messages regarding the *cron* system
Local0	Reserved for your use
Local1	Reserved for your use
Local2	Reserved for your use
Local3	Reserved for your use
Local4	Reserved for your use
Local5	Reserved for your use

Table 11-2. syslog facilities (continued)

syslog facility	Description
Local6	Reserved for your use
Local7	Reserved for your use (default Cisco log level)

Cisco routers are usually configured to use one of the reserved facilities *local0* through *local7*.

 The *syslog* server must be configured to receive and record the log messages to a file. On almost all Unix systems, the syslog configuration file is */etc/syslog.conf*. The standard format for *syslog.conf* files is (with tabs, not spaces):

```
Facility.Severity    logfile
```

If you are unfamiliar with *syslog*, the easiest way to get a router logging to the *syslog* server is to use a facility that is already configured. However, this facility mixes your Cisco log messages with server log messages. The recommended way to get the router logged into the server is to configure a unique facility, such as *local6* or *local7*, to send messages to a different file. For example, to configure the *syslog* server to send all log messages it receives that have a facility of *local6* and a severity of informational to the file */var/log/cisco*, your */etc/syslog.conf* file might contain:

```
local6.info        /var/log/cisco
```

You would then configure each router to use facility *local6* when sending messages to the *syslog* server.

Configuring syslog logging

To configure *syslog* logging on your router:

1. Configure the *syslog* facility using the *logging facility* command.
2. Configure the *syslog* severity level with the *logging trap* command.
3. Configure the *syslog* server to which log messages will be sent with the *logging* command.

To configure your router to send log messages to the server 13.18.10.4 using facility *local6* and severity *informational*:

```
RouterOne#config terminal
Enter configuration commands, one per line.  End with CNTL/Z.
RouterOne(config)#logging facility local6
RouterOne(config)#logging trap informational
RouterOne(config)#logging 13.18.10.4
RouterOne(config)#^Z
```

You can specify additional *syslog* servers with additional *logging <ip-address>* commands and specify that log messages will be sent to each server for redundancy.

By default, many *syslog* servers accept messages from any IP address. While this won't let an attacker modify log messages already recorded, it does allow an attacker to send bogus log messages that get mixed in with your good messages. It can also allow an attacker to use up all of the disk space on your *syslog* server so that valid log messages can't be recorded because of lack of space.

It is important to make sure your *syslog* server does not accept *syslog* messages from systems external to your network. This can be accomplished by using ACLs at your network boundaries to deny all incoming *syslog* packets (UDP port 514) and/or by configuring the *syslog* server to accept log messages only from your internal network.

syslog sequence numbers

Cisco has recently added a feature that stamp each *syslog* message with a sequence number. These numbers increase by one for each *syslog* message sent. These sequence number can provide a way for an administrator to determine whether the log files have been tampered with. A log file that is missing a set of sequence numbers indicates that the log files are either incomplete or have been tampered with. This example enables *syslog* sequence numbers:

```
RouterOne#config terminal
Enter configuration commands, one per line.  End with CNTL/Z.
RouterOne(config)#service sequence-numbers
RouterOne(config)#^Z
```

Sequence numbers do little if intruders accesses the *syslog* server—they can simply resequence the messages in the log file. However, sequence numbers can be useful in determining whether bogus messages are being forwarded to a *syslog* server. A log file that contains log messages without sequence numbers or with duplicate sequence numbers indicates that someone is sending bogus message to your *syslog* server.

Throttling syslog messages

IOS Version 12.1(3)T introduced the ability to limit the number of *syslog* messages sent to and from the router in a specific time frame. Some logging, such as ACL violation logging, if not implemented correctly, can cause the router to overwhelm the *syslog* server with thousands of messages a second. You can limit the number of messages sent with the *logging rate-limit* command. This example limits message output to 10 messages a second:

```
RouterOne#config terminal
Enter configuration commands, one per line.  End with CNTL/Z.
RouterOne(config)#logging rate-limit all 10
RouterOne(config)#^Z
```

You can append the *except* keyword followed by a severity level to rate-limit only low-priority messages.

For example, to avoid rate-limiting messages of severity *error* or higher, enter:

```
RouterOne#config terminal
Enter configuration commands, one per line.  End with CNTL/Z.
RouterOne(config)#logging rate-limit all 10 except error
RouterOne(config)#^Z
```

SNMP Traps

If you run SNMP (see Chapter 8), you can use SNMP traps to log additional information. Traps are packets sent to an SNMP server when specific events occur. Such events include high temperatures, configuration changes, and down interfaces. If you are familiar with SNMP and want to enable SNMP traps on your router, you must:

1. Use the *snmp-server host* command to configure which SNMP server will receive the traps.

2. Use the *snmp-server enable traps* command to enable SNMP traps.

The following example configures the router to send traps to the SNMP server 13. 145.6.5:

```
RouterOne#config terminal
Enter configuration commands, one per line.  End with CNTL/Z.
RouterOne(config)#snmp-server host 13.145.6.5 public
RouterOne(config)#snmp-server enable traps
RouterOne(config)#^Z
```

This example configures the router to send all possible traps to the SNMP server. You can supply additional arguments to the *snmp-server enable traps* command to limit the traps sent. See Cisco's documents on SNMP traps for more information.

ACL Violation Logging

Aside from system logging, ACL violation logging is an important area to configure. By logging ACL violations, you can record any time your ACLs block access. This is extremely useful for determining when attackers are trying to spoof, log in, or access your router from external or untrusted systems.

ACL violation logging can be enabled by simply adding the keyword *log* or *log-input* to the end of your ACL statements. Be selective about what you choose to log. Adding the *log* keyword to the wrong filters can end up logging every packet in and out of your networks.

The *log* keyword provides information on the type, date, and time of the ACL violation and is the only option for standard ACLs. The *log-input* keyword is available on extended ACLs and logs additional information about the input interface and source MAC address.

The *log* keyword works only for standard access lists. Both the *log* and *log-input* keywords can be used for extended and named ACLs.

Antispoofing Violations

The following examples configure your ACL antispoofing filters to log both inbound and outbound spoofing attempts. Assuming our internal network was 130.18.0.0/16, an ingress filter that logs all spoofed packets looks like:

```
RouterOne#config terminal
Enter configuration commands, one per line.  End with CNTL/Z.
RouterOne(config)#access-list 115 deny ip 130.18.0.0 0.0.255.255 any log-input
RouterOne(config)#access-list 115 permit ip any any
RouterOne(config)#^Z
```

This filter would be placed inbound on each interface that borders an external network. Assuming this was Serial 0/0 on *RouterOne*, enter:

```
RouterOne#config terminal
Enter configuration commands, one per line.  End with CNTL/Z.
RouterOne(config)#int Serial 0/0
RouterOne(config-if)#ip access-group 115 in
RouterOne(config-if)#^Z
```

An egress filter that logs all attempts at sending spoofed packets out of the network would look like:

```
RouterOne#config terminal
Enter configuration commands, one per line.  End with CNTL/Z.
RouterOne(config)#access-list 116 permit ip 130.18.0.0 0.0.255.255 any
RouterOne(config)#access-list 116 deny ip any any log-input
RouterOne(config)#^Z
```

And would be applied to all outgoing interfaces:

```
RouterOne#config terminal
Enter configuration commands, one per line.  End with CNTL/Z.
RouterOne(config)#int Serial 0/0
RouterOne(config-if)#ip access-group 116 out
RouterOne(config-if)#^Z
```

VTY Access Logging

Logging router login attempts through VTYs is very important. It can give you an early indication that someone is trying to access your router without authorization. Assuming you want only the IP 130.18.5.6 to be able to access the router through VTYs, your ACL would look like:

```
RouterOne#config terminal
Enter configuration commands, one per line.  End with CNTL/Z.
RouterOne(config)#access-list 117 permit ip host 130.18.5.6 any
RouterOne(config)#access-list 117 deny ip any any log-input
RouterOne(config)#^Z
```

You would apply it the VTY lines 0 through 4 with:

```
RouterOne#config terminal
Enter configuration commands, one per line.  End with CNTL/Z.
RouterOne(config)#line vty 0 4
RouterOne(config-line)#access-class 117 in
RouterOne(config-line)#^Z
```

Now someone from an unauthorized IP trying to access a router VTY will generate a log message. The following message is an sample log entry of an unauthorized person trying to telnet to the router:

```
Oct 13 21:10:44.185 EDT: %SEC-6-IPACCESSLOGP: list 120 denied tcp 19.8.59.41(63104) -
> 0.0.0.0(23), 1 packet
```

Many sites also choose to log all permitted VTY access attempts in addition to blocked access ones. Since all VTY access is through TCP, you can use the ACL keyword *established* to log successful access attempts without overwhelming your router or *syslog* server. This can be done effectively if you:

- Pass, without logging, all established TCP connections from permitted IPs.
- Pass and log the first packet for all TCP sessions from permitted IPs.
- Deny and log all other packets.

This example logs both access attempts from approved IPs and access attempts from unapproved IP addresses:

```
RouterOne#config terminal
Enter configuration commands, one per line.  End with CNTL/Z.
RouterOne(config)#access-list 117 permit tcp host 130.218.5.6 any established
RouterOne(config)#access-list 117 permit tcp host 130.218.5.6 any log-input
RouterOne(config)#access-list 117 deny ip any any log-input
RouterOne(config)#^Z
```

Other Services

Other protocols and services such as HTTP, SNMP, ICMP, and route filtering can be logged in the same way. Just add the keyword *log* or *log-input* to the deny statements of the ACLs for each service you want to log.

AAA Accounting

AAA accounting allows you to log additional information that cannot be obtained from the previous logging methods. Using Cisco's TACACS+, AAA accounting can log every command executed on the router to the Network Access Server (NAS).

AAA Accounting Methods

There are five methods of AAA accounting—EXEC, System, Command, Connection, and Network. Here is a short description of each method:

EXEC accounting
> EXEC accounting records information about each EXEC, or shell, session on the router. It records information such as username, date, time, and IP of the system connecting to the router.

System accounting
> System accounting logs information about system-level events, such as reboots or when accounting is turned on or off.

Command accounting
> Command accounting logs information about the commands typed at the EXEC shell prompt. It records information (including what command was executed, who executed the command, the privilege level, and the date and time). Please note that older versions of Cisco's implementation of RADIUS do not support Command accounting, so you will need to use TACACS+ or upgrade.

Connection accounting
> Connection accounting logs information about outgoing connections made from the router. These connections include telnet, rlogin, tn3270, and LAT.

Network accounting
> Network accounting logs information about PPP, SLIP, and ARAP sessions.

AAA Accounting Types

To log the largest amount of useful information, you should turn on accounting for all five methods. Each method supports three types of logging:

start-stop
> The *start-stop* keyword configures the router to generate a log message when a service starts and stops. For example, using the *start-stop* keyword for EXEC, accounting generates a log message when a user first accesses the router and another log messages when the user disconnects from the router.

stop-only
> The *stop-only* keyword configures the router to generate log messages only when a service ends. With EXEC accounting, this keyword generates log messages only when a user disconnects from the router.

wait-start
> The *wait-start* keyword delays the start of the requested service until confirmation is received from the NAS server that a log message has been received. This is typically reserved for higher-security installations that want to guarantee that each connection and command that run on a system is recorded. If the NAS

server doesn't indicate that it successfully received the log message, the router will not start the requested service or command.

AAA Accounting Configurations

Recommended initial settings for each method are shown in Table 11-3.

Table 11-3. Recommended AAA method types

Method	Recommended starting type	Explanation
EXEC	*start-stop*	This method makes determining exactly when someone accessed the router and exactly when they disconnected much easier.
System	*stop-only*	System messages are usually atomic events that don't need the start and stop times recorded. The *stop-only* keyword is usually sufficient for System accounting.
Command	*stop-only*	Commands are usually run in such short time periods that start and stop times are of limited use and can double the amount of log messages you have to analyze.
Connection	*start-stop*	Logging the start and stop times of outgoing connections from the router makes analyzing log files easier.
Network	*start-stop*	Again, logging start and stop times of these network connections makes log file analysis less of a chore and more intuitive.

The rest of this section provides examples on configuring each logging method.

Accounting with TACACS+

If you have AAA configured to use TACACS+, you can enable EXEC, System, Connection, and Network accounting to your NAS server with:

```
RouterOne#config terminal
Enter configuration commands, one per line.  End with CNTL/Z.
RouterOne(config)#aaa accounting exec default start-stop group tacacs+
RouterOne(config)#aaa accounting system default stop-only group tacacs+
RouterOne(config)#aaa accounting connection default start-stop group tacacs+
RouterOne(config)#aaa accounting network default start-stop group tacacs+
RouterOne(config)#^Z
```

To configure Command accounting, you also need to supply the privilege level you want logged. Unless you have changed the default privilege levels, privilege levels 1 and 15 should capture everything. If you have custom privilege-level configurations, make sure you add commands to log all levels you are interested in:

```
RouterOne#config terminal
Enter configuration commands, one per line.  End with CNTL/Z.
RouterOne(config)#aaa accounting commands 1 default stop-only group tacacs+
RouterOne(config)#aaa accounting commands 15 default stop-only group tacacs+
RouterOne(config)#^Z
```

Accounting with RADIUS

If you have AAA configured to use RADIUS, you can enable EXEC, System, Connection, and Network accounting to your NAS server with:

```
RouterOne#config terminal
Enter configuration commands, one per line.  End with CNTL/Z.
RouterOne(config)#aaa accounting exec default start-stop group radius
RouterOne(config)#aaa accounting system default stop-only group radius
RouterOne(config)#aaa accounting connection default start-stop group radius
RouterOne(config)#aaa accounting network default start-stop group radius
RouterOne(config)#^Z
```

You also need to enable Command accounting for all privilege levels you are interested in. Older versions of Cisco's IOS don't support Command accounting through RADIUS. If you determine that your router doesn't support RADIUS command logging, then either migrate to TACACS+ or upgrade your IOS:

```
RouterOne#config terminal
Enter configuration commands, one per line.  End with CNTL/Z.
RouterOne(config)#aaa accounting commands 1 default stop-only group radius
RouterOne(config)#aaa accounting commands 15 default stop-only group radius
RouterOne(config)#^Z
```

AAA authentication failure logging

AAA also needs to be configured to log authentication failures. The following example will generate an AAA log message each time someone attempts to access the router but fails:

```
RouterOne#config terminal
Enter configuration commands, one per line.  End with CNTL/Z.
RouterOne(config)#aaa accounting send stop-record authentication failure
RouterOne(config)#^Z
```

Logging Checklist

This checklist summarizes the important security information presented in this chapter. A complete security checklist is provided in Appendix A.

- Actively monitor all logs for indications of attacks, misconfigurations, and failures.
- Configure logging timestamps to include milliseconds using the *service timestamp log datetime msec localtime* command.
- Enable RAM buffer logging with the *logging buffered* command. The default and recommended level is 6 (informational).
- Enable logging sequence numbers with the *service sequence-numbers* command.
- Configure routers to send log messages to a *syslog* server to preserve the messages:
  - Make sure that sites requiring higher levels of security and auditability send router log messages to multiple *syslog* servers for redundancy.

— Filter out *syslog* messages from external systems through ACLs at your network's border or with the *syslog* server itself.

- Configure key ACLs to record access violations. Recommended ACL logging includes:
  - Antispoofing violations
  - VTY access attempts
  - HTTP access attempts
  - SNMP access attempts
  - Route filter violations
  - ICMP violations
  - Any other important filters
- In environments requiring additional security, use AAA and enable AAA accounting:
  - Configure EXEC, System, Connection, and Network accounting to record information on system events and user sessions.
  - Configure AAA accounting to record authentication failures.
  - If a record of each command executed on the router is required, configure command accounting.

Checklist Quick Reference

You can use this checklist in two ways. First, you can use it as a checklist when securing your routers. You can also use the checklist as the basis for auditing the security of your routers.

Hardening Your Routers

If you are using this checklist to harden your routers, a good approach is to use the following three-step process:

1. Use the checklist to determine your routers' current security level. Check off each item that has already been taken care of.

2. Review all items in the checklist that have not been checked off. For each item, determine how you are going to address that issue—secure it, leave it alone and accept the risk, or assign the risk to someone else (e.g., insurance).

3. Secure each item that you determined needs securing. For all other items, document why you are leaving this item unsecured. It is important to list the risks associated with the item and determine why the risk can be ignored or how it is being assigned to someone else.

For example, if your network has two routers and one administrator, the cost associated with setting up an AAA server is probably not justifiable. Local usernames and passwords would be much more reasonable. Documenting these decisions and getting management to sign off on them helps to cover your tail when an incident occurs.

Auditing Your Routers

Auditing is a topic for a book unto itself and generally requires a higher skill level than hardening. When hardening a router, a sysadmin can usually turn off services that aren't understood. An auditor, however, must understand not only how each service works, but also the risks associated with that service. For those who are not just hardening their routers, but auditing them, this checklist can serve as the foundation for an audit of Cisco router security. For those new to auditing, here is an overview of the typical auditing process:

Securing approval to perform the audit

When performing an audit, make sure you have not only the approval, but also the authority, to perform the audit. Without approval and authority the best-case scenario is an incomplete and useless audit. Since many security audits can look like attacks, the worst-case scenario is your termination or incarceration.

Planning the audit

Make sure that the scope and focus of the audit are defined and agreed upon. This is the time to define what resources will be needed for the audit, how the audit will be performed, and what the deliverables will be.

Performing the audit

Performing the audit usually takes two very different steps. First, interviews are done with everyone involved with items being audited. For a router, this might include managers responsible for overseeing the router administrators, the information security officer of the organization, the senior network administrator, the junior sysadmins responsible for day-to-day maintenance, and, depending on where the router is located, janitors or computer operations personnel who have access to the room the router is in. Second, the router must be audited technically. The technical audit is when you analyze router configurations and possibly perform penetration testing against the organization's routers.

Reporting the audit

The report details the findings of the audit and highlights the strengths and weaknesses discovered in the audit. Circulation of security audit reports should be restricted since they probably contain vulnerability information.

Following up the audit

Finally, the organization that receives the audit report should review the report and, for each weakness uncovered, take action to correct the weakness, decide that the weakness is considered an acceptable risk and live with it, or assign the risk to a third party with outsourcing or insurance.

Here are some standard points that are key to performing an effective audit:

Independence

The ideal auditor is usually a third party with no vested interest in the outcome of the audit. When network administrators audit their own networks, it becomes too easy to selectively ignore certain weaknesses. Also, many managers seem to see a direct correlation between how much they pay for information and how much they believe it. Independent audits can often open management's eyes to the problems that insiders can't push politically. This can often help administrators get the resources they really need.

Competence

An auditor must be competent to perform the audit. Auditors need the skills and knowledge to understand how administrators interact with their routers and to unravel all the nuances of Cisco router configuration files.

Ethics

In security, ethics is always very high on the list of requirements. Since the purpose of auditing is to uncover weakness and vulnerabilities, an auditor must have impeccable ethics, both personally and professionally.

Due diligence

Auditors must not only have the knowledge to perform the audit, but also must be able to demonstrate and document that they performed their work to a professionally acceptable level. The auditor must be competent and must also understand professional auditing standards to the point at which an audit by a different professional would not uncover significant omissions in the original audit. A knowledgeable but lazy auditor can do more harm than good.

Finally, many audits are performed to test compliance with existing security policies. The following checklist can be very useful in establishing or updating these policies.

Cisco Router Security Checklist

This section provides a complete list of the checklists shown at the end of most chapters. It is only a guideline; you don't have to agree with or implement each of the recommendations. If the checklist gets you to think about and address each issue, it has served its purpose. As an administrator, you are responsible for working with management, determining how much risk your organization can handle, and knowing how secure your routers need to be.

IOS Security (Chapter 2)

- Make sure that all routers are running a current IOS.
- Make sure that the IOS version is in General Deployment (unless all risks with the non-GD IOS version have been addressed).
- Check the IOS version against existing Cisco Security Advisories.
- Regularly check Cisco Security Advisories for IOS vulnerabilities.

Basic Access Control (Chapter 3)

- Secure physical access to the router. (See Appendix B).
- Secure console access with the *login* and *password* commands.
- Disable or secure AUX access with the *login* and *password* commands.
- Disable or secure all VTY access with the *login* and *password* commands.

- Do not use the *no login* command under any line (*con/aux/vty*) configurations.
- Set the enable password using the *enable secret* command.
- In organizations in which multiple administrators access a router, enable accountability by requiring administrators to have separate accounts to access the router. This can be accomplished through local usernames or more centralized methods involving network access servers.
- Do not use TACACS and Extended TACACS in favor of TACACS+, RADIUS, or Kerberos.
- If any version of TACACS is used for user-level authentications, set the method of last resort to the privileged password (set with *enable secret*) and not to default to open access with no authentication.
- Do not use standard TACACS for privileged-level access.
- If any version of TACACS is used for the enable password—privileged-level access—then set the method of last resort to the enable secret password and not to automatically succeed.
- Make sure the router does not use TFTP to automatically load its configuration at every reboot. If it must, then harden and secure the TFTP server.
- Do not configure the router to serve as a TFTP server.
- With dial-up access to the router, make sure both the AUX port and the modem are password protected.
- With dial-up access to the router, configure callback security to a predefined number, or make sure the telephone company uses a closed user group to restrict which numbers are allowed to call your modems.
- Never connect a modem to the console port.
- Disable reverse Telnet to all physical ports.
- Disable Telnet in favor of SSH on all VTY lines.
- If insecure protocols such at Telnet or HTTP must be used, use IPSec to encrypt all vulnerable traffic.
- Make sure all VTY access uses ACLs to restrict access to a few secured IPs.
- Set the *exec-timeout* on all VTYs to five minutes or less.
- Enable the global command *service tcp-keepalives-in*.
- Disable HTTP access to the router.
- If HTTP access must be used:
    — Limit its use to secure networks.
    — Only use it over IPSec.
    — Restrict access with ACLs to a few secured IPs.
    — Change the HTTP authentication method from the default enable password.

Password Security (Chapter 4)

- Enable *service password-encryption* on all routers.
- Set the privileged-level (level 15) password with the *enable secret* command and not with the *enable password* command.
- Make sure all passwords are strong passwords that are not based on English or foreign words.
- Make sure each router has different enable and user passwords.
- Keep backup configuration files encrypted on a secure server.
- Access routers only from secure or trusted systems.
- In large organizations with numerous personnel with router access, use additional privilege levels to restrict access to unnecessary commands.
- Reconfigure the *connect*, *telnet*, *rlogin*, *show ip access-lists*, *show access-lists*, and *show logging* commands to privilege level 15.

AAA Security (Chapter 5)

- If AAA is used, when possible, use TACACS+ instead of other methods.
- If TACACS+ or RADIUS is used, then keep the configuration files secure, since TACACS+ and RADIUS keys are not obscured by the *service password-encryption* command.
- If AAA authentication is used, always set the backup method for authentication to locally configured usernames or the default privileged password and never to none.
- If AAA authorization is used and your security needs are low to medium, make sure the backup method for authorization is *if-authenticated* (to avoid being locked out of the router).
- If AAA authorization is used and you need a higher level of security, make sure there is no backup method for authorization.
- Disable HTTP access. If it must be used, make sure it uses TACACS+ or RADIUS, and not the default privileged-mode password, for authentication.
- In larger organizations that need dual-factor access control, configure the router's TACACS+ or RADIUS servers to use token-based access control.

Warning Banners (Chapter 6)

- Make sure every router has an appropriate warning banner that includes wording that states:
  - The router is for authorized personnel only.
  - The router is for official use only.

- — Users have no expectations of privacy.
- — All access and use may (not will) be monitored and/or recorded.
- — Monitoring and/or recording may be turned over to the appropriate authorities.
- — Use of the system implies consent to the previously mentioned conditions.
- Make sure the banner does not say *Welcome* anywhere in it.
- Make sure the banner does not include any identifying information relating to the router, the administrators, or the organization running the router.
- Check local legal requirements to make sure the banner contains all necessary language and content.
- Use the *banner login* command to display the banner every time a user attempts to log in.
- Use the *banner exec* command to display the banner a second time every time a user starts an EXEC or shell prompt.

Unnecessary Protocols and Services (Chapter 7)

- Disable the following services on every interface on every router:
  - — Disable sending ICMP redirects with the *no ip redirects* command.
  - — Disable ICMP broadcasts with the *no ip directed-broadcast* command.
  - — Disable ICMP mask replies with the *no ip mask-reply* command.
  - — Disable ICMP unreachables with the *no ip unreachables* command.
  - — Disable Proxy ARP with the *no ip proxy-arp* command.
- Disable CDP globally with the *no cdp run* command or disable it on each interface with the *no cdp enable* command.
- Disable source routing with the *no ip source-route* command.
- Disable small services with the *no service tcp-small-servers* and the *no udp-small-servers* commands.
- Disable Finger with the *no service finger* command.
- Severly restrict incoming ICMP packets using an appropriate ACL. (Ideally, only MTU discovery is allowed between your internal network and external networks.)
- Disable miscellaneous services such as *BOOTP*, PAD, configuration autoloading, and DNS.
- Disable or secure HTTP access (see Chapter 3).
- Disable or secure SNMP access (see Chapter 8).

SNMP Security (Chapter 8)

- Disable SNMP, if it is not needed.
- Use different community or authentication strings for each router, if possible. (This often become unmanageable.)
- Make sure community strings and passwords are well chosen and not easily guessed.
- Restrict all SNMP access to specific hosts through ACLs.
- Restrict all SNMP output through the use of views.
- Disable read/write SNMP access unless absolutely necessary.
- If SNMP read/write access is configured, use the *snmp-server tftp-server-list* command to restrict SNMP-controlled TFTP transfers.
- Disable SNMP v1 and v2c in favor of SNMP v3.
- Under SNMP v3:
  — Make sure that SNMP v1 and v2c are disabled.
  — Use both authentication and encryption (*AuthPriv*) on your routers.
  — Use views to limit SNMP access to information.
- Secure all SNMP Management Servers.

Routing Protocol and Antispoofing (Chapter 9)

- Take antispoofing measures at each router bordering an external network:
  — Enable *ip verify unicast reverse-path* on all interfaces that connect with external networks and are not involved in asymmetrical routing.
  — If uRPF cannot be used (or additional logging is required), apply antispoofing ingress and egress ACLs to all interfaces that connect to an external network.
  — If your network is very small and you need additional security, consider using static routes.
- When using a routing protocol, choose one that supports authentication and enable authentication on all routers on the network:
  — Choose the authentication password well and make sure controls are in place to keep the authentication passwords secret.
  — Use secure hash protocols such as MD5, not plain-text protocols, for authentication.
- Use route filters at the border between your network and the networks controlled by others to prevent false routing information from being injected into your network.

NTP Security (Chapter 10)

- Make sure all routers use NTP to synchronize their time.
- On larger networks requiring more accurate time, use redundant timeservers and synchronize routers to multiple servers to prevent a single point of failure.
- Use the *ntp master* command only when external time synchronization is not possible—i.e., in networks not connected to the Internet.
- Make sure all routers have ACLs preventing them from becoming public time synchronization servers. These ACLs should restrict what servers the router synchronizes to and systems the router will synchronize.
- Use NTP authentication between clients, servers, and peers to ensure that time is synchronized to approved servers only.

Logging (Chapter 11)

- Actively monitor all logs for indications of attacks, misconfigurations, and failures.
- Configure logging timestamps to include milliseconds using the *service timestamp log datetime msec localtime* command.
- Enable RAM buffer logging with the *logging buffered* command. The default and recommended level is 6 (informational).
- Enable logging sequence numbers with the *service sequence-numbers* command.
- Configure routers to send log messages to a *syslog* server to preserve the messages:
  - Make sure that sites requiring higher levels of security and auditability send router log messages to multiple *syslog* servers for redundancy.
  - Filter out *syslog* messages from external systems through ACLs at your network's border or with the *syslog* server itself.
- Configure key ACLs to record access violations. Recommended ACL logging includes:
  - Antispoofing violations
  - VTY access attempts
  - HTTP access attempts
  - SNMP access attempts
  - Route filter violations
  - ICMP violations
  - Any other important filters
- In environments requiring additional security, use AAA and enable AAA accounting:
  - Configure EXEC, System, Connection, and Network accounting to record information on system events and user sessions.

— Configure AAA accounting to record authentication failures.

— If a record of each command executed on the router is required, configure command accounting.

Physical Security (Appendix B)

- Make sure all routers are in a secured area:
  - Make sure walls continue below raised flooring.
  - Make sure walls continue above dropped/false ceilings.
  - Make sure air ducts are too small to be used for access.
- Make sure the only access into the area is through locked doors:
  - Make sure there are a minimum number of doors into the secured area.
  - Make sure all doors and door frames are metal.
  - Make sure all doors are self-closing with no feature to hold them open.
  - Make sure all doors remained locked at all times.
- Make sure all doors have adequate locks.
- Choose appropriate locks—keyed, mechanical, electronic, carded, biometric, or dual-factor.
- Allow only required and authorized personnel to access the secure location.
- Keep router configuration backups in a separate and secure area.
- Make sure the area has adequate fire prevention controls:
  - Make sure multiple smoke alarms are in the secured area.
  - Make sure automatic fire suppression controls are adequate.
  - Provide easily accessable manual fire extinguishers in and near the room.
  - Do not store or keep flammable material in the room.
- Adequately protect the area against water damage:
  - Make sure no water or steam pipes run through the room.
  - If a sprinkler system is present, make sure the room is equipped with a drain.
  - If a sprinkler system is present, tie its activation into the circuit breaker to shut off all equipment if the sprinkler system activates.
- Adequately protect the area against excessive heat:
  - Make sure there is adequate air-conditioning to keep the room around 69 to 75 degrees Fahrenheit.
  - Make sure all equipment fans and ventilation areas are free from obstruction.
- Make sure he secured area has adequate humidity control to keep the room around 40 to 60 percent humidity.

- Adequately protect the area against electrical damage:
  - — Make sure all equipment is on an uninterruptible power supply.
  - — Make sure the flooring is anti-static electricity flooring.
- Free the area from excessive airborne dust and dirt.
- Clear and unclog equipment fans, filters, and vents.

Incident Reponse (Appendix C)

- Follow your established incident response plan, if you have one.
- Determine if the problem was due to an accident or malicious attack.
- While determining the cause of the problem:
  - — Change nothing.
  - — Record everything.
- If you don't have an incident response policy and you determine you have been hacked, touch nothing and call law enforcement.
- If you cannot call or wait for law enforcement, understand the risks you take by modifying or rebooting the router.
- If you must modify or reboot the router, first record all volatile evidence from the router in a well-documented manner.
- Recover from the incident by getting the router functional again.
- Perform a postmortem and implement changes to prevent future compromises.
- If you don't have a documented and tested incident response plan, develop one now.

Physical Security

Physical security has been around since the first caveman guarded his mammoth skins and clubbed his neighbor over the head for trying to steal them. Because of its long history, physical security is a very mature field. However, as many *InfoSec* professionals start out as technicians, this aspect of security is often overlooked. In most circumstances, security is completely compromised once physical access is achieved. With physical access, attackers can disable, reconfigure, replace, and/or steal systems. Security is only as strong as the weakest link, and no amount of firewall protection, intrusion detection, or network security does any good if an attacker can simply walk off with the system. This appendix discusses how to physically protect routers from attackers, Murphy's Law, and Mother Nature.

Protection Against People

The first denial-of-service attack against a network probably consisted of cola being poured into a router. Using a baseball bat would be equally effective. Without physical security, a janitor tripping over a power cord can bring down an entire network. Physical security not only protects against maliciousness, but also stupidity. Physical access is used not just for destruction. With physical access, attackers can take control of your systems. With physical access, it takes only a few minutes for an attacker to perform a password recovery on a Cisco router. Sophisticated attackers wouldn't even bother with password recovery. To avoid minutes of downtime and possible detection, they would replace the router with one that had been preconfigured to function normally, but to also let them record traffic and access trusted networks.

Location

The first aspect to discuss when talking about physical security is location. Where are the routers physically located? Do they sit in a secured room, in a closet down the hall, or somewhere up in the suspended ceiling? Because of their importance, routers should always be kept in a secure location. How secure depends on the size of the organization and the value of the traffic passing over the network. Routers should always sit in a locked room. Ideally, this room is occupied by computer equipment only, and not by people. Keeping the equipment separate allows the room to be optimized for the equipment rather than the comfort of people, makes it easier to limit the number of people who have access to the room, and makes installation of a fire suppression system easier and cheaper.

A secure location provides good access control. The only way in or out of the room should be through the doors. This may sound obvious, but often a room that can be accessed under raised floors, over dropped ceilings, or through air ducts is chosen. Make sure that if the room has a raised floor, all the walls continue down below the raised floor; if it has dropped or false ceilings, all the walls continue up above the dropped ceiling; and that any air ducts into the room are too small to be used for access.

Doors

A minimum number of doors should open into the secure area. The fewer the number of access points, the easier access can be controlled. All doors, however, should generally be of the same type and use the same type of access control mechanism. Different methods of access into the same room can become an administration nightmare and, by making things more complex, increase the risk of compromise.

Many doors are hollow wood doors with wooden door frames. One swift kick is usually all that is needed to bypass one of these doors. Both the door and door frame to the secured area should be made of metal.

All doors should be self-closing and remain locked at all times. Additionally, the doors should not have mechanisms that prop them open. Even in the most secure area, there seems to be a great temptation to prop open doors. This happens most often when someone needs to make frequent trips to and from the room or when a vendor needs access and the door is propped open to provide this access. Anytime the door to a secure area is unlocked or propped open, the equipment in the room is vulnerable. Making matters worse, people often forget that they unlocked a door or propped it open, which can lead to days or weeks of vulnerability.

Locks

You can choose from hundreds of locks to secure a room. These range from the basic keyed entry to dual card-swipe/keycode-access locks. Each lock has its own strengths and weaknesses, so choosing a lock for a secured area depends on the needs of the organization. The "key" (pun intended) is to use the lock that best fits the needs and culture of an organization. The foundations for access control rest on three criteria— something a person has, something a person knows, or something a person is. A regular house key would be an example of something a person has. Anyone who physically has the house key can use it to enter the house. A keycode is an example of something a person knows. Anyone who knows the code can use it to open the door. A fingerprint or iris scan is an example of something a person is. Access is granted only to individuals with a specific fingerprint or iris pattern. The most effective, and most expensive, access controls combine at least two of these criteria.

Keyed locks

Keyed locks are the most common types of locks and range from the small locks on suitcases to the dual keys required to open safe deposit boxes. These locks are examples of access control based on something a person has and they require a physical key with specific ridges and valleys in order to open. The advantages to keyed locks are that they do not require electricity to work, are easy to use, and do not require user training—everyone knows how to use a key to open a door. A disadvantage of keyed locks is that if a single key is compromised, the lock and all other keys must be physically replaced. Additionally, there is no logging inherent to the use of keys. If ten people have keys to the server room, after an incident there is no way to know which of the ten accessed the room.

Mechanical locks

Mechanical locks are locks that use mechanical push-button codes to allow entry. These locks are based on something a person knows rather than something one has (like an actual key). The advantages are that they do not require electricity to run, can be reprogrammed without the need to replace hardware, and are very easy to use. The disadvantages are that these locks rely on one code to provide access and provide no logging to show who accessed the room. If a code is compromised, the lock can easily be reset to use another code; however, the reliance on a single code for all personnel means that, similarly to a keyed entry, there is no way of knowing who entered the room at a specific day and time.

Electronic locks

Electronic locks are similar to mechanical locks because they also require a specific keycode in order to get access. Likewise, they are based on something a person knows. Electronic locks, however, allow the use of different key codes for each individual. Therefore, they provide the ability to log individual access based on key codes. Additionally, these locks are usually very easy to change in the event of a compromise. Unlike mechanical locks, if a single code is compromised, then only that code has to be reset and changed, avoiding the need to reset and redistribute everyone's code (as with mechanical locks). These locks however, rely on electricity to function. Some state or cities may require by law that electronic locks open automatically if electricity is removed. This is a significant security problem and should be researched before you decide to implement electronic locks. On the positive side, electronic locks require very little electricity to function, and most come with batteries to allow them to function even in the event of a power failure.

Card-access locks

Similar to keyed locks, card-access locks are based on something a person has. These locks require users to have a card preprogrammed with their access information. The locks have embedded card readers that read the key cards. The advantages of card-access locks are numerous. Individual locks can be programmed to allow access to individual users as needed, and reprogramming these locks does not require the replacement of any physical items. These locks can also keep access logs that include the identity of the person and the date and time he or she accessed the room. A disadvantage of these locks is the reliance on only a key card. An attacker needs to steal or compromise only one key card in order to gain access. Another disadvantage of these locks is that they rely on electricity and are subject to the same restrictions as mentioned earlier for electronic locks.

Biometric locks

Biometric locks are different from our previous locks because they grant access based on something a person is rather then something they have or know. Generally, it is much more difficult to fake this type of credential than it is to fake the previous two. James Bond aside, fingerprint and iris pattern scanning can provide a high level of identity verification. There are many types of biometric locks. In addition to finger-prints and iris patterns, biometric locks can use voice recognition, finger length and hand geometry, retina scanning, handwriting recognition, and even typing pattern recognition. Each of these technologies has it own strengths and weaknesses. The ideal biometric system is difficult to fool—voice recordings and photographs won't fool it, it's noninvasive—it doesn't shoot a laser into the eye to scan the retina, and it's relatively inexpensive. Currently, fingerprint and iris pattern recognition generally meet these requirements the best.

Dual-factor locks

Dual-factor locks are locks that combine two of the previous locks into one. With single-factor locks, if any access method is compromised, access is compromised. For example, if someone steals the code to a mechanical or electronic lock, he can use that code to gain entry. Worse, he can publish that code on the Internet, and anyone who downloads the code can gain entry. Dual-factor locks help prevent this single point of failure; they require two of the three access criteria before granting access. A lock that requires a key card and a code is an example of a dual-factor lock. Such a lock would require use of a key card—something he has—and then a code—some-thing he knows—before granting access. A card or code by itself is useless, and if one is compromised, access is still secure. Another example of a dual-factor lock would be one that requires a retina scan—something a person is—and a key card—some-thing a person has—before granting access. Dual-factor locks are more expensive to purchase and maintain, but make it exponentially harder for an attacker to gain access to a secured area.

Personnel

Billions of dollars are spent annually to protect organizations from hackers on the Internet, yet an estimated 70 percent of attacks come from insiders. The personnel responsible for an organization's routers necessarily have physical access to them. Recognizing this problem, many organizations are performing background checks on all personnel responsible for the administration and maintenance of critical systems. The problem is that many organizations do not realize that other forgotten personnel may have access to rooms that hold server and network equipment.

Often, network equipment is located in the same rooms as telephone equipment. In many organizations, telephone company personnel are granted complete and instant access to any room housing telephone equipment. Are all personnel claiming to be telephone company personnel really from the telephone company? Most janitorial staff have master keys allowing them to clean every room in a building. Do they also have access to the company's network closets? Finally, building maintenance personnel also often have master keys allowing them access to all rooms in a building. Do the maintenance personnel ever prop open doors for convenience?

When determining who has access to secured areas, it is important to consider not only the personnel under an administrator's control, but also the invisible support staff such as telephone technicians, janitors, and maintenance people. All it takes is one of these people to be overly trusting or susceptible to bribes, and all physical access can be compromised.

Backups

Backups are considered necessary protection against hardware failure (Murphy). Backups are not often considered a part of information security, which can cause severe compromises. Organizations spend hundreds of thousands of dollars protecting themselves from the Internet, while an attacker can walk off with a copy of their backup tapes.

Make sure you keep backup copies of router configurations. Occasionally, even the best-intentioned router technician blows away a router configuration; more often, a hardware failure results in a lost configuration. With backups, restoring a router can take minutes. Without backups, restoring a router can take hours or days, depending on the level of network documentation. Inevitably, most networks without router configuration backups are the same ones with poor documentation.

In addition to the need to keep backups of router configurations, good security requires that these configurations be kept in a secure location. This means a secure physical location. Many people new to information security question this point and ask, "Wouldn't encryption be good enough?" In response, encryption would help, but it is still no replacement for physical security. The next question is inevitably "Why?"

Assume that critical information, such as router configurations, is kept encrypted on a network administrator's PC located inside a cubicle. Sound secure? With physical access to that PC, it is trivial to use a keystroke recorder to intercept the encryption key. Once the key is compromised, with physical access, an attacker can either steal or copy the backup configurations and decrypt them. Physical security for backups should be given as much thought as the physical security of the routers themselves.

Protection Against Murphy and Mother Nature

Availability is inherent to information security's CIA triad. In order to ensure network availability, good security protects not only against physical compromise by people, but also disasters. These disasters can range from earthquakes to flooding to fire. Additionally, these disasters do not have to be natural. An old and effective denial-of-service attack is to simply use arson and burn down a building.

Fire

Fire is usually considered one of the most probable disasters. Fire damage has been around for thousands of years and is of serious concern whether started accidentally or purposefully. Fire is such a concern that everywhere in the United States, proper fire detection and prevention controls are required before an organization can get property insurance.

Each area with critical routers should have both fire detection and prevention methods. Multiple smoke alarms will ensure a warning in case one alarm fails. Fire extinguishers rated for electrical fires should be obvious and easily accessible near the secured area. Flammable materials should be kept to a minimum. This often means storing manuals in another location or a closed metal cabinet. Finally, adequate automatic fire suppression methods should be employed. Both water and gas have unique advantages and disadvantages, though water suppression methods are usually cheaper and can be safe and effective when linked with a breaker that cuts power to the room before the sprinkler system is activated.

Water

Water can be severely damaging to electronic equipment such as routers. Therefore, rooms containing network equipment should not have water or steam pipes running through them. If either of these pipes leaks or breaks, it can cause irreparable damage to electrical equipment.

Most network equipment rooms are equipped with sprinkler systems rather than gas suppression. Sprinkler systems can be safe and effective, provided adequate caution is taken. Sprinkler systems can be broken down into three main types—wet pipe, dry pipe, and hybrid. Which one of these you choose depends on your budget and needs.

In wet pipe systems, water is already inside all fire suppression pipes running through the room. Each pipe has multiple sprinkler heads, and each head is triggered individually by excessive heat—normally around 150 degrees Fahrenheit. The advantage to this system is its immediate response; the water is already in the pipe, and the sprinkler heads are triggered only in areas in which fire is detected. The disadvantage is having water in overhead pipes. If any of these pipes leak or break, it will damage the electronic equipment in the room.

In dry pipe systems, the fire suppression pipes are normally dry and free of water. The water is stopped at a main release valve before it enters the room. This release valve is connected to the fire detection alarms, and if an fire is detected, the valve releases water into the pipes, providing fire suppression for the entire room. The advantage of this system is that the overhead pipes do not continuously contain water, eliminating the risk of leaks and breaks. However, there is a delay in suppression after a fire is detected since time is needed to flood the pipes with water. Another disadvantage is that dry pipe systems provide fire suppression for the entire room, rather than just the area where a fire has been detected. This can increase the amount of damaged equipment, since everything is doused with water.

Hybrid systems attempt to combine the advantages of the wet pipe and dry pipe systems. Hybrid systems use a main release valve to keep pipes dry. However, these systems also employ individually activated sprinkler heads as in the wet pipe systems. Once a fire is detected, the pipes are flooded, but water is released only onto areas in which the sprinkler heads are triggered by excessive heat. These systems, while more expensive, provide a good compromise between area protection and not having water constantly in the pipes overhead.

Finally, to minimize damage, rooms using water for fire suppression should be equipped with drains, and the activation of the sprinkler system should be directly connected to a circuit breaker for the room. This connection should automatically flip the breaker and shut off electrical power to the room whenever the sprinkler system is activated. Once the routers are dry and clean, they can then be powered on again.

Heat

Heat is another enemy of computer equipment. Excessive heat, excepting a fire, does not cause immediate equipment failure, but drastically shortens the life of electronic equipment. Heat can be a hidden problem since the temperature inside routers can often be 20 degrees Fahrenheit hotter than the room. With such a difference, heat-induced failures can still occur in a cool room. To help keep the internal temperature of routers at a safe level, the ambient room temperature should be between 69 and 75 degrees Fahrenheit. Additionally, all equipment should have unobstructed ventilation for all fans, filters, and heat syncs. These precautions can significantly lengthen the life of routers and network equipment.

Humidity

Uncontrolled humidity can also shorten the life of computer equipment. In low-humidity conditions, static electricity can become a serious problem. In dry air conditions, static shocks can reach several thousand volts—enough to damage most computer circuits. Excessive humidity can also cause problems. In high-humidity conditions, metal connectors start a process similar to electroplating that causes them to loose conductivity and cement connectors into their sockets.

Humidity levels should be kept between 40 and 60 percent. A note of caution, however: humidity control systems require drains to get rid of excessive humidity and a water line to add humidity when it is too low. Care should be taken to make sure that there is minimal chance that water from the humidity control system will make contact with network equipment. Finally, in no case should the system cause condensation to occur on the electronic equipment.

Electricity

By definition, lectronic equipment runs on electricity. The general reliability of modern electrical power makes it easy to forget the need for protection against spikes, surges, sags, and outages. Electrical protection falls into three major categories: line conditioners, uninterruptible power supplies, and backup power sources.

Power line conditioners are used to smooth out voltage irregularities such as spikes, surges, and sags. Surge protection power strips act as partial line conditioners by protecting against voltage spikes and surges; however, they generally do not protect against power sags.

Uninterruptible power supplies (UPSs) include batteries to replace failed AC power, and UPSs provide excellent protection against short-term power outages. While normal power is functioning, UPSs charge their internal batteries, and if the power sags or goes out completely, they power equipment from their batteries. Most modern UPSs also include spike and surge protection and act as line conditioners in addition to providing backup electricity.

Backup power sources are required when primary power is unavailable for extended periods of time and are usually run by either gasoline or diesel fuel. Backup power systems can power equipment directly or can maintain the charge in UPS batteries.

Basic electrical protection involves the use of power strips and UPSs to provide short-term protection against short-term power problems. In critical areas, a backup power generator should be employed to protect against longer power outages.

Dirt and Dust

In the past, dust and contaminants in the air were a serious problem, and computer room air needed to be purified. Most modern systems, however, have hermetically sealed disk drives, and modern media are much less vulnerable to damage and contamination from dust particles. The main danger from airborne dirt and dust today comes from clogged ventilation. When a system's fans, filters, vents, or heat syncs become clogged with dust, they lose the ability to circulate cooling air through the system. This causes internal temperatures to remain high, significantly shortening the life of the equipment. Because many network rooms are unfinished, dust can be particularly heavy; it is extremely important to regularly clean the ventilation of these systems.

Physical Security Checklist

- Make sure all routers are in a secured area:
  - Make sure walls continue below raised flooring.
  - Make sure walls continue above dropped/false ceilings.
  - Make sure air ducts are too small to be used for access.
- Make sure the only access into the area is through locked doors:
  - Make sure there are a minimum number of doors into the secured area.
  - Make sure all doors and door frames are metal.
  - Make sure all doors are self-closing with no feature to hold them open.
  - Make sure all doors remained locked at all times.
- Make sure all doors have adequate locks.
- Choose appropriate locks—keyed, mechanical, electronic, carded, biometric, or dual-factor.
- Allow only required and authorized personnel to access the secure location.
- Keep router configuration backups in a separate and secure area.
- Make sure the area has adequate fire prevention controls:
  - Make sure multiple smoke alarms are in the secured area.
  - Make sure automatic fire suppression controls are adequate.
  - Provide easily accessable manual fire extinguishers in and near the room.
  - Do not store or keep flammable material in the room.
- Adequately protect the area against water damage:
  - Make sure no water or steam pipes run through the room.
  - If a sprinkler system is present, make sure the room is equipped with a drain.
  - If a sprinkler system is present, tie its activation into the circuit breaker to shut off all equipment if the sprinkler system activates.

- Adequately protect the area against excessive heat:
  - Make sure there is adequate air-conditioning to keep the room around 69 to 75 degrees Fahrenheit.
  - Make sure all equipment fans and ventilation areas are free from obstruction.
- Make sure he secured area has adequate humidity control to keep the room around 40 to 60 percent humidity.
- Adequately protect the area against electrical damage:
  - Make sure all equipment is on an uninterruptible power supply.
  - Make sure the flooring is anti-static electricity flooring.
- Free the area from excessive airborne dust and dirt.
- Clear and unclog equipment fans, filters, and vents.

Incident Response

Your router has been hacked. Now what? This chapter covers the basics of emergency response when dealing with a router compromise. Ideally, you should have an incident response plan that is tailored to your organization. If you are reading this chapter because you have just been hacked and don't know what to do, first promise that as soon as this incident is over, you will develop a complete incident response plan. Then keep reading for help on responding to incidents involving router compromises.

The goals of incident response are to:

- Determine if the incident is an attack or an accident
- Discover what happened and the scope of the incident
- Preserve all the evidence
- Recover from the incident
- Take the steps necessary to prevent this incident from happening again

Warning!

If you do not have a detailed incident response plan in place and you have been hacked, it is best to do nothing yourself and to call law enforcement. They are trained to preserve the evidence and investigate the incident and can track down attackers through means you don't have access to. Therefore, the first recommendation is to *do nothing and call law enforcement*.

However, many attacks may look like accidental outages (and vice versa). The following information is provided for those who are still trying to determine if an incident is due to a hacker or an accident or for those who must get the compromised router operational as soon as possible. So please read this entire chapter—especially the section on preserving evidence—to collect enough evidence to provide law enforcement with leads if necessary. When you reconfigure or reboot the router, you destroy the original evidence, so how you make copies of this evidence is extremely important to having any chance of holding up in a court of law.

Keys to Investigating

Your mission while investigating an incident is to:

1. Change nothing.
2. Record everything.

Even if you suspect the incident was accidental, it is best to follow these two rules until you are sure. Once you start modifying your router, you destroy your ability to use any information on it in the future.

Change Nothing

Many administrators' first step when a router goes down is to reboot the system. It is amazing how many times this seems to fix a problem, but if the router malfunctioned because of an attack by a hacker, rebooting the system can cause the loss of valuable evidence, sometimes all evidence of the attack. Additionally, while investigating the incident, until you have determined that it was indeed an accident, do not make any changes to the router. These changes can cause significant problems if the evidence is ever needed in court.

Record Everything

The most unobtrusive way to log into a router is through the console port. Thus, for investigation purposes, use terminal emulation software—like HyperTerminal—to connect to the router's console port. Before you even log in, configure your terminal emulation software to capture your current session. This will record everything you do and can be helpful in proving that you did not make any changes to the router during your investigation. HyperTerminal can be configured to capture your session though the menu option Transfer → Capture Text. This option will bring up a dialog box that lets you choose the name and location of the capture file. Once you have chosen it, click the Start button to begin recording. You can now log into the router and use read-only commands—*show* commands—to investigate the incident.

 Make sure you record the date and time inside your terminal session somehow. To do this, right after you connect to the router, run the *show clock* command. Run this command about every five minutes or so to establish a time record, and then run it one more time just before you log out of the router.

Attack Versus Accident

When many administrators start getting involved in information security, they tend to get very worried and excited about the state of their networks. First, they get worried because they realize how vulnerable their systems are; second, they get excited by the challenge of protecting those systems. The Holy Grail for many system and network administrators who move into *InfoSec* is catching the bad guy. This provides the ability to impress friends with tales of how your cunning outsmarted the wily hacker.

This excitement can make these administrators jump to conclusions and see accidental incidents as attacks. In their excitement, they inform management that the systems have been hacked, and they are quickly tracking down the attacker. This can become embarrassing when it turns out that the janitor accidentally tripped over a power cord.

So, before you run to management claiming that you have been hacked, take the time to rule out accidental causes. They are more often responsible for router problems than are intentional compromises, and caution can save you much embarrassment.

Discover What Happened and the Scope of the Incident

People request a nice checklist when they reach the step of determining what happened and how big the problem is. Networks are so complex and types of attacks are changing so fast that such a checklist will never exist. This type of work is what separates those who truly understand routers and networking from those who don't. To determine what happened, you need to go through your router logs, configurations, access points, and so on. Once you decide that your router was actually compromised by an attacker, you need to determine details such as:

- What parts of your organization are impacted, and how much damage is the impact causing?
- How did the attacker do it?
- Who is the attacker?
- Is the incident ongoing, or has it stopped?
- What other systems or routers have been accessed from the compromised router?
- What version of IOS are you running, and are there any known vulnerabilities to this version?
- What IP addresses have recently accessed the router?
- Have the *running-config* or *startup-config* been changed?

This list is far from complete, but will hopefully get you thinking in the right direction. More often than not, answering every question on this list necessarily involves law enforcement. If you are not sure how to start looking for answers to the preceding questions, you are probably over your head and it is time to call in a professional.

Evidence Preservation

If you must get your router functional as quickly as possible, it is vitally important that you record any volatile information that may be lost upon reconfiguration or reboot of the router. Before you make any changes to, shut down, or reboot the router, follow these steps to gather as much of this volatile evidence as possible:

1. Connect to the router's console port. This is the least-intrusive way to access the router. It doesn't require network access and will not tip off your attackers if they are sniffing your network.
2. Configure your terminal emulation software to record your session.
3. Log in to the router.
4. Enter enable mode (*enable*).
5. Show the current date and time (*show clock detail*).
6. Write down the time from a trusted time source—atomic clock, NTP server, etc.
7. Show the IOS, uptime, and hardware information (*show version*).
8. Show the current running configuration (*show running-config*).
9. Show the current startup configuration (*show startup-config*).
10. Show scheduled reload time (system may auto reboot, if set) (*show reload*).
11. Show the routing tables (*show ip route*).
12. Show the ARP tables (*show ip arp*).
13. Show who is logged in (*show users*).
14. Show current logs (*show logging*).
15. Show current interface ip configuration (*show ip interface*).
16. Show current interface configuration (*show interfaces*).
17. Show TCP connections (*show tcp brief all*).
18. Show open sockets (*show ip sockets*).
19. Show NAT translations (*show ip nat translations verbose*).
20. Show NetFlows (*show ip cache flow*).
21. Show CEF forwarding table (*show ip cef*).
22. Show SNMP v3 users (*show snmp user*).
23. Show SNMP v3 groups (*show snmp group*).
24. Show date and time again (*show clock detail*).
25. Write down the time from a trusted time source again.
26. Disconnect from the router.

27. End your terminal recording session.

28. Print out your recording session.

29. Write the two times you recorded from the trusted time source on the printout.

30. Sign and date the printout.

31. Get a witness to sign and date the printout.

32. Keep both the electronic copy and the hardcopy in a secure location until you can turn them over to law enforcement.

Next, you need to gather information from the router externally:

1. Port scan the router from an external system.

2. Record the time of the port scan from a trusted time source.

3. Print out the port scan and write the time on the printout.

4. If the router is running SNMP, get a copy of the current SNMP tree. This can be done with a command such as *snmpwalk* (from NetSNMP *http://net-snmp. sourceforge.net*).

5. Record the time of the SNMP walk from a trusted time source.

6. Print out the SNMP tree info and write the time on the printout.

7. Sign and date both printouts.

8. Get a witness to sign and date both printouts.

9. Keep all copies in a secure location until you can turn them over to law enforcement.

 A good source of accurate time is a portable clock that has a built-in radio receiver and synchronizes itself with US atomic clocks. They can usually be purchased for less than $50.

The worst-case scenario is when the router's *enable* password has been changed by either an accident or an attacker. In these situations your ability to collect forensic information is severely limited. Password recovery procedures require rebooting the router, which destroys much of the evidence you are interested in. If this happens, attempt to log in with a lower privileged account and run as many of the preceding commands as possible. When you cannot log into the router at all, the information gathered externally becomes much more important because it is all you have. Therefore, be sure to try to use SNMP and port scans to gather as much information about the router as possible.

Recovering from the Incident

Once law enforcement officials have completed their initial analysis of the router, they may return it to you or keep it for more detailed forensic investigation. Whether you are using the original router or a replacement router, the next step is to recover from the incident. This is why it is so important to have current documentation on your network and backup copies of all your router configuration files. With backup copies, recovery may be as simple as reloading the backup configuration onto the router. However, this configuration has already been compromised once; it is imperative that you move on to the next step—preventing future incidents.

Preventing Future Incidents

Having finally recovered, your job isn't over. In the course of your response and investigation, you should have determined how the attacker compromised your router. Chances are it will have been compromised due to a known vulnerability that hadn't been patched, an attacker sniffing the wire for passwords, or poorly chosen router passwords that the attacker simply guessed.

Whatever the cause, now is the time to do a postmortem and come up with a plan to close the security hole and prevent such holes from appearing in the future. Finally, if you responded to this incident by the seat of your pants, consider this your wake-up call and develop a documented and tested incident response policy.

Incident Response Checklist

Here is a quick overview of responding to an incident:

- Follow your established incident response plan, if you have one.
- Determine if the problem was due to an accident or malicious attack.
- While determining the cause of the problem:
    — Change nothing.
    — Record everything.
- If you don't have an incident response policy and you determine you have been hacked, touch nothing and call law enforcement.
- If you cannot call or wait for law enforcement, understand the risks you take by modifying or rebooting the router.
- If you must modify or reboot the router, first record all volatile evidence from the router in a well-documented manner.
- Recover from the incident by getting the router functional again.
- Perform a postmortem and implement changes to prevent future compromises.
- If you don't have a documented and tested incident response plan, develop one now.

Configuration Examples

This appendix consolidates many of the concepts presented in this book into example router configurations that can be used as templates for your Cisco routers. While these examples don't include all possible configurations, they do include the most common security configurations for both small and large organizations. The examples are created so you can type all commands directly into your router. They will be slightly different than a *show running-config* because of IOS version differences and command line differences.

Basic Example Configuration

This is a basic secure configuration that you might find at an organization with a small network with few routers and few administrators. In addition to standard security settings, this configuration will:

- Disable all unneeded services. This configuration doesn't use HTTP, SNMP, TFTP, CDP, etc.
- Configure the router to use an external NTP server to set its time, while peering with two other routers—10.10.2.1 and 10.10.4.1. NTP is configured to use authentication and to serve only clients on the internal network.
- Configure logging to log to the *syslog* server 10.10.4.6.
- Enable an external interface—Serial 0/0—that has antispoofing ACL applied to it. This interface uses BGP, with authentication, as its routing protocol.
- Enable an internal interface—Fast Ethernet 0/0—that has been configured to use RIP v2, with authentication, as its routing protocol.
- Configure console access to use a line password for authentication.
- Disable AUX access.
- Restrict VTY access to the IP 10.10.4.10 and configure it to use only SSH:

```
!
! Enable password encryption
```

```
service password-encryption
!
! Set the privileged level password
enable secret SecretEnablePassword
!
! Disable Global services & protocols
no service udp-small-servers
no service tcp-small-servers
no service finger
no service pad
no service config
no boot network
no cdp run
no snmp-server
no ip bootp server
no ip source-route
no ip finger
no ip name-server
no ip classless
no ip http server
!
! Enable needed services
ip cef
service tcp-keepalives-in
!
! Configure the Loopback Address
int loopback 0
  ip address 10.10.10.1 255.255.255.252
!
! Configure NTP
  ! Use External Server 192.5.5.250
  ntp server 192.5.5.250 prefer
  ! Set our NTP source address to be our loopback interface
  ntp source loopback 0
  ! Enable NTP Authentication
  ntp authenticate
  ! Create & Trust our NTP authentication Key
  ntp authentication-key 10 md5 SecretNtpKey
  ntp trusted-key 10
  ! Now Peer with our other main routers (10.10.2.1 & 10.10.4.1)
  ! But use the authentication key we just created
  ntp peer 10.10.2.1 key 10
  ntp peer 10.10.4.1 key 10
  ! Configure NTP to only peer with our main routers (10.10.2.1 & 10.10.4.1)
    ! Create ACL & Log violations
    access-list 20 permit host 10.10.2.1
    access-list 20 permit host 10.10.4.1
    access-list 20 deny any log
    ! Apply the ACL as our peer ACL
    ntp access-group peer 20
  ! Configure NTP to only serve our internal networks 10.10.0.0/16
    ! Create and ACL & Log violations
    access-list 21 permit 10.10.0.0 0.0.255.255
    access-list 21 deny any log
    ! Apply the ACL as our server-only ACL
```

```
    ntp access-group serve-only 21
 ! Only server 20 NTP clients maximum
 ntp max-associations 20
 ! Set to Eastern Daylight Savings Time
 clock summer-time EDT recurring
!
! Set up logging
 ! Turn logging on
 logging on
 ! Configure logging to use millisecond time stamps and the timezone
 service timestamps log datetime msec localtime show-timezone
 ! Enable sequence numbers and throttle messages below error level
 service sequence-numbers
 logging rate-limit all 10 except error
 ! Create our logging buffer
 logging buffer 32000
 ! Set out logging buffer to see notification level messages & above
 logging buffer notification
 ! Disable Console logging
 no logging console
 ! Configure logging to go to our syslog server 10.10.4.6
 logging 10.10.4.6
 ! Set our syslog facility to local6 and our level to informational & above
 logging facility local6
 logging trap informational
!
! NSA recommended command privilege changes
 privilege exec level 15 connect
 privilege exec level 15 telnet
 privilege exec level 15 rlogin
 privilege exec level 15 show ip access-lists
 privilege exec level 15 show access-lists
 privilege exec level 15 show logging
 privilege exec level 1 show ip
!
! Configure the Login Banner
 banner login ^C
 WARNING!!!
 This system is solely for the use of authorized users for official purposes.
 You have no expectation of privacy in its use and to ensure that the system
 is functioning properly, individuals using this computer system are subject
 to having all of their activities monitored and recorded by system
 personnel.  Use of this system evidences an express consent to such
 monitoring and agreement that if such monitoring reveals evidence of
 possible abuse or criminal activity, system personnel may provide the
 results of such monitoring to appropriate officials.
 ^C
!
! Configure the EXEC Banner
 banner exec ^C
 NOTICE!!!
 This system is solely for the use of authorized users for official purposes.
 You have no expectation of privacy in its use and to ensure that the system
 is functioning properly, individuals using this computer system are subject
```

to having all of their activities monitored and recorded by system
personnel. Use of this system evidences an express consent to such
monitoring and agreement that if such monitoring reveals evidence of
possible abuse or criminal activity, system personnel may provide the
results of such monitoring to appropriate officials.

```
^C
!
! Configure BGP for our ISP link using authentication
router bgp 100
  network 10.10.2.0
  network 10.10.4.0
  network 130.18.6.0
  neighbor 130.18.6.2 remote-as 115
  neighbor 130.18.6.2 password SecretBGPpassword
!
! Create an Ingress (incoming) ACL for our External Interface (Serial 0/0)
  ! Anti-spoofing (Internet Network is 10.10.0.0/16)
  access-list 101 deny ip 10.10.0.0 0.0.255.255 any log-input
  access-list 101 deny ip 127.0.0.0 0.255.255.255 any log-input
  access-list 101 deny ip 10.0.0.0 0.255.255.255 any log-input
  access-list 101 deny ip 172.16.0.0 0.15.255.255 any log-input
  access-list 101 deny ip 192.168.0.0 0.0.255.255 any log-input
  access-list 101 deny ip 224.0.0.0 15.255.255.255 any log-input
  access-list 101 deny ip 240.0.0.0 7.255.255.255 any log-input
  ! Block all incoming Syslog packets (port 514)
  access-list 101 deny udp any any eq 514 log-input
  ! Block incoming all incoming ICMP packets except MTU discovery
  ! This won't allow us to ping or traceroute outside our network
  access-list 101 permit icmp any any 3 4
  access-list 101 deny icmp any any log-input
  ! Allow everything else
  access-list 101 permit ip any any
!
! Create our Egress filter to no allow our network to send out spoofed packets
access-list 102 permit ip 10.10.0.0 0.0.255.255 any
access-list 102 deny ip any any log-input
!
! External Interface (Directly connected to Internet)
interface Serial 0/0
  ip address 130.18.6.1 255.255.255.252
  ! Disable unneeded protocols & services
  no ip redirects
  no ip directed-broadcast
  no ip mask-reply
  no ip unreachables
  no ip proxy-arp
  no cdp enable
  ! Enable uRPF anti-spoofing features
  ip verify unicast reverse-path
  ! Make sure we don't serve as a NTP server
  ntp disable
  ! Apply our ingress (incoming) ACL
  ip access-group 101 in
  ! Apply our egress (outgoing) ACL
  ip access-group 102 out
```

```
!
! Configure RIPv2 for our internal networking
router rip
  version 2
  network 10.0.0.0
!
! Define a Key Chain for our RIPv2 authentication
key chain 10
  key 1
    key-string SecretRipKey
!
! Internal Interface FastEthernet 0/0 (connected our Internal network)
interface FastEthernet 0/0
  ip address 10.10.2.2 255.255.255.0
  ! Disable unneeded protocols & services
  no ip redirects
  no ip directed-broadcast
  no ip mask-reply
  no ip unreachables
  no ip proxy-arp
  no cdp enable
  ! Enable uRPF anti-spoofing features
  ip verify unicast reverse-path
  ! Enable & Configure RIP v2 authentication
  ip rip authentication key-chain 10
  ip rip authentication mode md5
!
! Securely Configure the Console
line con 0
  ! Enable logins
  login
  ! Set the Console Login password
  password SecretConsolePassword
  ! Disable all network access
  transport input none
!
! Disable the AUX port
line aux 0
  ! Use the login and no password commands to disable access
  login
  no password
  ! Disable all network access
  transport input none
  ! NSA's other recommended commands for disabling access
  no exec
  exec-timeout 0 1
!
! Enable SSH on the router
  ! Give the router a hostname
  hostname RouterOne
  ! Configure our domain
  ip domain-name Company.Com
  ! Configure our RSA keys
  !crypto key generate rsa
```

```
! Configure a local username for vty SSH access
username JohnDoe password PasswordForJohnDoe
! Configure SSH retries & Timeout
ip ssh time-out 60
ip ssh authenication-retries 2
!
! Create ACL to restrict VTY access managers IP only (10.10.4.10)
access-list 15 permit 10.10.4.10
access-list 15 deny any log
! Configure & Secure VTY access
line vty 0 4
   ! Enable login using the locally define username and password
   login local
   ! Make sure we only use SSH to access the router
   transport input ssh
   ! Set the timeout to 5 minutes
   exec-timeout 5 0
   ! Apply ACL to restrict VTY access
   access-class 15 in
```

AAA Example Configuration

This configuration is the same as the preceding one, except that instead of local and line authentication, it uses AAA authentication and a TACACS+ access control server. The TACACS+ server used in this example has the IP address 10.10.2.20.

```
!
! Enable password encryption
service password-encryption
!
! Set the privileged level password
enable secret UnGuessablePassword
!
! Disable Global services & protocols
no service udp-small-servers
no service tcp-small-servers
no service finger
no service pad
no service config
no boot network
no cdp run
no snmp-server
no ip bootp server
no ip source-route
no ip finger
no ip name-server
no ip classless
no ip http server
!
! Enable needed services
ip cef
service tcp-keepalives-in
```

```
!
! Configure the Loopback Address
int loopback 0
  ip address 10.10.10.1 255.255.255.252
!
! Configure NTP
  ! Use External Server 192.5.5.250
  ntp server 192.5.5.250 prefer
  ! Set our NTP source address to be our loopback interface
  ntp source loopback 0
  ! Enable NTP Authentication
  ntp authenticate
  ! Create & Trust our NTP authentication Key
  ntp authentication-key 10 md5 SecretNtpKey
  ntp trusted-key 10
  ! Now Peer with our other main routers (10.10.2.1 & 10.10.4.1)
  ! But use the authentication key we just created
  ntp peer 10.10.2.1 key 10
  ntp peer 10.10.4.1 key 10
  ! Configure NTP to only peer with our main routers (10.10.2.1 & 10.10.4.1)
    ! Create ACL & Log violations
    access-list 20 permit host 10.10.2.1
    access-list 20 permit host 10.10.4.1
    access-list 20 deny any log
    ! Apply the ACL as our peer ACL
    ntp access-group peer 20
  ! Configure NTP to only serve our internal networks 10.10.0.0/16
    ! Create and ACL & Log violations
    access-list 21 permit 10.10.0.0 0.0.255.255
    access-list 21 deny any log
    ! Apply the ACL as our server-only ACL
    ntp access-group serve-only 21
  ! Only server 20 NTP clients maximum
  ntp max-associations 20
  ! Set to Eastern Daylight Savings Time
  clock summer-time EDT recurring
!
! Set up logging
  ! Turn logging on
  logging on
  ! Configure logging to use millisecond time stamps and the timezone
  service timestamps log datetime msec localtime show-timezone
  ! Enable sequence numbers and throttle messages below error level
  service sequence-numbers
  logging rate-limit all 10 except error
  ! Create our logging buffer
  logging buffer 32000
  ! Set out logging buffer to see notification level messages & above
  logging buffer notification
  ! Disable Console logging
  no logging console
  ! Configure logging to go to our syslog server 10.10.4.6
  logging 10.10.4.6
  ! Set our syslog facility to local6 and our level to informational & above
  logging facility local6
```

```
    logging trap informational
!
! NSA recommended command privilege changes
privilege exec level 15 connect
privilege exec level 15 telnet
privilege exec level 15 rlogin
privilege exec level 15 show ip access-lists
privilege exec level 15 show access-lists
privilege exec level 15 show logging
privilege exec level 1 show ip
!
! Configure the Login Banner
banner login ^C
WARNING!!!
This system is solely for the use of authorized users for official purposes.
You have no expectation of privacy in its use and to ensure that the system
is functioning properly, individuals using this computer system are subject
to having all of their activities monitored and recorded by system
personnel.  Use of this system evidences an express consent to such
monitoring and agreement that if such monitoring reveals evidence of
possible abuse or criminal activity, system personnel may provide the
results of such monitoring to appropriate officials.
^C
!
! Configure the EXEC Banner
banner exec ^C
NOTICE!!!
This system is solely for the use of authorized users for official purposes.
You have no expectation of privacy in its use and to ensure that the system
is functioning properly, individuals using this computer system are subject
to having all of their activities monitored and recorded by system
personnel.  Use of this system evidences an express consent to such
monitoring and agreement that if such monitoring reveals evidence of
possible abuse or criminal activity, system personnel may provide the
results of such monitoring to appropriate officials.
^C
!
! Configure BGP for our ISP link using authentication
router bgp 100
  network 10.10.2.0
  network 10.10.4.0
  network 130.18.6.0
  neighbor 130.18.6.2 remote-as 115
  neighbor 130.18.6.2 password SecretBGPpassword
!
! Create an Ingress (incoming) ACL for our External Interface (Serial 0/0)
  ! Anti-spoofing (Internet Network is 10.10.0.0/16)
  access-list 101 deny ip 10.10.0.0 0.0.255.255 any log-input
  access-list 101 deny ip 127.0.0.0 0.255.255.255 any log-input
  access-list 101 deny ip 10.0.0.0 0.255.255.255 any log-input
  access-list 101 deny ip 172.16.0.0 0.15.255.255 any log-input
  access-list 101 deny ip 192.168.0.0 0.0.255.255 any log-input
  access-list 101 deny ip 224.0.0.0 15.255.255.255 any log-input
  access-list 101 deny ip 240.0.0.0 7.255.255.255 any log-input
```

```
! Block all incoming Syslog packets (port 514)
access-list 101 deny udp any any eq 514 log-input
! Block incoming all incoming ICMP packets except MTU discovery
! This won't allow us to ping or traceroute outside our network
access-list 101 permit icmp any any 3 4
access-list 101 deny icmp any any log-input
! Allow everything else
access-list 101 permit ip any any
!
! Create our Egress filter to no allow our network to send out spoofed packets
access-list 102 permit ip 10.10.0.0 0.0.255.255 any
access-list 102 deny ip any any log-input
!
! External Interface (Directly connected to Internet)
interface Serial 0/0
  ip address 130.18.6.1 255.255.255.252
  ! Disable unneeded protocols & services
  no ip redirects
  no ip directed-broadcast
  no ip mask-reply
  no ip unreachables
  no ip proxy-arp
  no cdp enable
  ! Enable uRPF anti-spoofing features
  ip verify unicast reverse-path
  ! Make sure we don't serve as a NTP server
  ntp disable
  ! Apply our ingress (incoming) ACL
  ip access-group 101 in
  ! Apply our egress (outgoing) ACL
  ip access-group 102 out
!
! Configure RIPv2 for our internal networking
router rip
  version 2
  network 10.0.0.0
!
! Define a Key Chain for our RIPv2 authentication
key chain 10
  key 1
    key-string SecretRipKey
!
! Internal Interface FastEthernet 0/0 (connected our Internal network)
interface FastEthernet 0/0
  ip address 10.10.2.2 255.255.255.0
  ! Disable unneeded protocols & services
  no ip redirects
  no ip directed-broadcast
  no ip mask-reply
  no ip unreachables
  no ip proxy-arp
  no cdp enable
  ! Enable uRPF anti-spoofing features
  ip verify unicast reverse-path
```

```
! Enable & Configure RIP v2 authentication
ip rip authentication key-chain 10
ip rip authentication mode md5
!
! THIS IS WHERE DIFFERENCES FROM PREVIOUS CONFIG START
! THIS CONFIG USES AAA INSTEAD OF LOCAL & LINE AUTHENTICATION
! IT ALSO USES AAA TO USE A TACACS+ SERVER FOR AUTHORIZATION.
!
! Enable AAA
 ! Define a new AAA model
 aaa new-model
 ! Define where to find our TACACS+ server (10.10.2.20)
 tacacs-server host 10.10.2.20
 ! Configure our TACACS+ server key
 tacacs-server key TACACSserverKEY
 ! Define default AAA authentication methods for logins:
 ! First TACACS+ server, then local usernames if server is unreachable
 aaa authentication login default group tacacs+ local
 ! Define default AAA authentication methods for enable password:
 ! First TACACS+ server, then local enable password if server is unreachable
 aaa authentication enable default group tacacs+ enable
 !
 ! Configure router to use AAA for authorization (Leave this part out if you
 ! only want to use AAA for authentication and keep standard authorization.
 !
 ! Configure AAA to use TACACS+ for EXEC (shell) authorization
 aaa authorization exec default group tacacs+ if-authenticated
 ! Configure AAA to use TACACS+ for level 1 and level 15 command authorization
 aaa authorization commands 1 default group tacacs+ if-authenticated
 aaa authorization commands 15 default group tacacs+ if-authenticated
 !
 ! Configure the router to use AAA to log to the TACACS+ server.
 !
 ! Configure the router to perform EXEC, System, Network & Connection logging
 ! to the TACACS+ server
 aaa accounting exec default start-stop group tacacs+
 aaa accounting system default stop-only group tacacs+
 aaa accounting connection default start-stop group tacacs+
 aaa accounting network default start-stop group tacacs+
 ! Now configure the router to log all level 1 (user) and level 15 (privilege)
 ! command the the TACACS+ server
 aaa accounting commands 1 default stop-only group tacacs+
 aaa accounting commands 15 default stop-only group tacacs+
!
! Securely Configure the Console
line con 0
 ! Configure the console to use the AAA method 'default' for authentication
 login authentication default
 ! Disable all network access
 transport input none
!
! Disable the AUX port
line aux 0
```

```
! Use the login and no password commands to disable access
login
no password
! Disable all network access
transport input none
! NSA's other recommended commands for disabling access
no exec
exec-timeout 0 1
!
! Enable SSH on the router
! Give the router a hostname
hostname RouterOne
! Configure our domain
ip domain-name Company.Com
!  Configure our RSA keys
!crypto key generate rsa
!  Configure a local username for vty SSH access
username JohnDoe password PasswordForJohnDoe
!  Configure SSH retries & Timeout
ip ssh time-out 60
ip ssh authenication-retries 2
!
! Create ACL to restrict VTY access managers IP only (10.10.4.10)
access-list 15 permit 10.10.4.10
access-list 15 deny any log
! Configure & Secure VTY access
line vty 0 4
    ! Configure logins to use the AAA methods 'default' for authentication.
    login authentication default
    ! Make sure we only use SSH to access the router
    transport input ssh
    ! Set the timeout to 5 minutes
    exec-timeout 5 0
    ! Apply ACL to restrict VTY access
    access-sclass 15 in
```

SNMP Example Configuration

The previous examples have SNMP turned off. If your organization requires SNMP, add the following configuration examples to the preceding ones. To enable this SNMP read-only access to the router, replace the *no snmp-server* command in the previous examples with the following configurations.

SNMP Version 2c

The following example configuration configures the router to provide SNMP v2c read-only access to the SNMP management system 10.10.4.10:

```
!
! Create an ACL that only allows 10.10.4.10 to use SNMP access
access-list 30 permit 10.10.4.10
```

```
access-list 30 deny any log
!
! Enable the SNMP read only server
snmp-server community SNMPreadOnlyCommunityString RO 30
```

SNMP Version 3

This example uses SNMP v3 authentication and encryption to protect SNMP traffic between the management server and the router and allows only SNMP management system 10.10.4.10 to access the router through SNMP:

```
!
! Create ACL that only allows 10.10.4.10 to use SNMP access
access-list 40 permit 10.10.4.10
access-list 40 deny any log
! Create an SNMP v3 group to use Authentication & Encryption
snmp-server group AuthPrivGroup v3 priv access 40
! Define and SNMPv3 user, authentication password, and encryption password.
snmp-server user MyUser3 AuthPrivGroup v3 auth md5 AuthPass priv des56 PrivPass
```

HTTP Configuration

If you decide that HTTP's usefulness outweighs its security problems, replace the *no ip http server* command in the preceding examples with the following. This example configures HTTP access for the IP 10.10.4.10 only:

```
!
! Create an ACL to limit HTTP access to 10.10.4.10
access-list 45 permit 10.10.4.10
access-list 45 deny any log
! Configure HTTP access to use the ACL
ip http access-class 45
! Configure HTTP access to use local authentication
ip http authentication local
!
```

Resources

This appendix lists resources that you may find useful when securing your routers, systems, and networks. It also provides links to sites where you can find more detailed information on topics that are out of the scope of this book—including IPSec, RADIUS/TACACS+, and intrusion detection.

Web Sites

http://www.cisco.com
> This site provides the most current information on Cisco routers and products. Cisco's online technical documentation is excellent and should usually be the first stop for questions involving Cisco routers.

http://www.cisco.com/go/psirt
> A direct link to Cisco's Product Security Incident Response Team (PSIRT) and a list of all Cisco IOS vulnerabilities.

http://www.cisco.com/cgi-bin/Support/FeatureNav/FN.pl
> Cisco's feature navigator. It helps determine what IOS versions and hardware support features such as IPSec and SSH.

http://nsa1.www.conxion.com/cisco
> NSA-recommended guides for securing Cisco routers.

http://nsa1.www.conxion.com
> Additional NSA-recommended security guides.

http://www.securityfocus.com
> A security site with excellent news, articles, tools, and vulnerability listings. SecurityFocus is also home to the *Bugtraq* vulnerability forum.

http://www.cert.org
> The original Computer Emergency Response Team (CERT) based out of Carnegie Mellon. CERT is an excellent resource on vulnerabilities, fixes, and incident response.

http://www.sans.org

The System Administrator and Network Security web site. It is an excellent source for research and education in the area of information security.

http://www.gocsi.com

The Computer Security Institute web site. he source of the annual FBI/CSI computer crime and security survey.

http://web.mit.edu/kerberos/www

The MIT Kerberos web site.

http://www.de.easynet.net/tacacs-faq

The TACACS frequently asked questions web site (with a focus on Cisco).

http://www.ietf.org/html.charters/OLD/radius-charter.html

The IETF RADIUS workgroup with links to RFCs and RADIUS information.

http://www.ietf.org/html.charters/ipsec-charter.html

The IETF IPSec working group page with links to IPSec drafts and RFCs.

http://www.rfc-editor.org

A site where you can search RFCs by number, topic, and keyword.

http://www.simpleweb.org

A site with links to more information about SNMP.

http://net-snmp.sourceforge.net

A web site for the Net-SNMP open source SNMP server and client software.

http://www.liquifried.com/docs/security/reservednets.html

A large listing of IANA-reserved networks that can be included in antispoofing filters.

http://www.ietf.org/html.charters/syslog-charter.html

The IETF *syslog* working group with links to drafts and RFCs.

http://www.isaca.org

The Information Systems Audit and Control Association web site. This organization sponsors the Certified Information Systems Auditor (CISA) certification.

Books

Boney, James. *Cisco IOS in a Nutshell*. O'Reilly & Associates, 2001.

This book consolidates the most important commands and features of IOS into a single volume.

Garfinkel, Simson and Gene Spafford. *Practical Unix and Internet Security*, Second Edition. O'Reilly & Associates, 1996.

This classic reference is the definitive source of information on securing both standalone Unix systems and those connected to the Internet.

Kaeo, Merike. *Designing Network Security*. Cisco Press, 1999.

Cisco's book on the fundamentals of Cisco network security.

Norberg, Stefan. *Securing Windows NT/2000 Servers for the Internet*. O'Reilly & Associates, 2000.

This concise guide simplifies the job of securing a Windows server by paring down installation and configuration instructions into a series of checklists.

Schneier, Bruce. *Applied Cryptography*. John Wiley & Sons, 1995.

An excellent reference and introduction to cryptography and standard encryption techniques and formulas.

Sedayao, Jeff. *Cisco IOS Access Lists*. O'Reilly & Associates, 2001.

This book focuses on a critical aspect of the Cisco IOS—access lists, which are central to securing routers and networks.

van Wyk, Kenneth and Richard Forno. *Incident Response*. O'Reilly & Associates, 2001.

This book combines technical information with guidelines for administrative planning so that organizations can map out their responses to computer incidents.

Wenstrom, Michael. *Managing Cisco Network Security*. Cisco Press, 2001.

Cisco's overview of network security using Cisco products by Cisco Systems

Zwicky, Elizabeth, Simon Cooper, and Brent Chapman. *Building Internet Firewalls*, Second Edition. O'Reilly & Associates, 2000.

An excellent book on the complexities of designing and building firewalls.

Index

We'd like to hear your suggestions for improving our indexes. Send email to *index@oreilly.com*.

encryption
    configuration files, 36
    MD5 hash algorithm, 32
    packets, SNMP v3, 76
    passwords, 32
    service password-encryption
        command, 33
    SNMP v3, 70
    strong encryption, MD5, 35
    Vigenere, 32
ethics, auditing and, 125
evidence preservation, incident
        response, 146
example configurations
    AAA, 154–159
    basic, 149–154
    HTTP, 160
    SNMP, 159
Exec accounting, AAA accounting
        method, 119
EXEC authorization, TACACS+, 46
EXEC banner, 56
exec-mode callback, 21
exec-timeout command, 26

F

FBI warning banner example, 54
filters
    antispoofing, 83–87
    route filtering, 92, 93
        global, 93
        network borders, 94
        per-interface filtering, 94
finger service, 64
fire, physical security and, 138
firewalls, source routing and, 63
flat structure configuration, NTP, 99–100
flowcontrol command, 22
footprinting, 2

G

GD (General Deployment) release, operating
        system, 6, 7
    naming scheme, 9
General Deployment, IOS Major Releases, 8
general logging practices, 108
global route filtering, 93
groups, Trusted groups, 79

H

hacks
    attacking other sites, 4
    disabled network, 3
    internal system attack, 3
    rerouting traffic, 4
    risk of attack, 4
    (see also attacks)
hardening routers
    checklist for process, 123
    defined, 1
heat, physical security, 139
hierarchical model configuration, NTP, 100
hijacking, remote administration and, 20
HTTP (Hypertext Transfer Protocol), 26
    access control, 12
    authentication, 27
    configuration example, 160
    limiting access, 27
    RADIUS authentication, 49
    security and, 65
    TACACS+ authentication and, 46
humidity, physical security and, 140
hybrid sprinkler systems, physical
        security, 139
HyperTerminal, 144

I

ICMP (Internet Central Message Protocol)
    directed broadcasts, 60
    information requests, 63
    mask reply, 61
    MTU discovery, 58
    redirects, 59
    timestamps, 63
ICMP unreachables, 62
IDS (intrustion detection system), 3
incident response
    attacks versus accidents, 145
    change nothing rule, 144
    checklist, 148
    evidence preservation, 146
    investigation checklist, 145
    law enforcement and, 143
    prevention, 148
    record everything rule, 144
    recovery, 147
    terminal emulation software and, 144
independence, auditing and, 124
information requests, ICMP, 63

About the Author

Thomas Akin is a Certified Information Systems Security Professional (CISSP) with a decade of experience in information security. He is the founding director of the Southeast Cybercrime Institute at Kennesaw State University, where he also serves as chairman of the Institute's Board of Advisors. He is an active member of the Attorney General's Georgia Cybercrime Task Force and heads its education committee. Heavily involved in Atlanta's InfoSec community, Thomas spends much of his time teaching, writing, and trying to keep his security, network, and Unix certifications up to date. Finally, he is the owner of and principal consultant for CrossRealm Consulting. More information about Thomas can be found at *http://www.crossrealm.com*.

Colophon

Our look is the result of reader comments, our own experimentation, and feedback from distribution channels. Distinctive covers complement our distinctive approach to technical topics, breathing personality and life into potentially dry subjects.

The animal on the cover of *Hardening Cisco Routers* is a North African wild ass. This mammal, an ancester of the domestic donkey, once lived in the Moroccan Atlas Mountain range and possibly throughout North Africa. The small population of wild asses is now confined to Sudan, Somalia, and Ethiopia.

Adapted to arid grasslands, the North African wild ass eats thorny, dry plants and grass. It retreats to rocky areas for shade during the hot, sunny hours of the day and is active in the early morning, at dusk, and at night. The wild ass needs water every two to three days and lives alone or temporarily in small groups of offspring to conserve food and water. Males generally live alone, especially when defending territory that contains sources of water.

The North African wild ass is in grave danger of extinction. Domestication, breeding with domestic animals, hunting, and competition with other animals (including humans) for water has diminished the population to a few hundred. Well-meaning tourists who chase the animals for photographs often exhaust the wild asses to the point of death. The animal is now one of the rarest mammals in the world, despite conservation efforts.

Ann Schirmer was the production editor and proofreader, and Norma Emory was the copyeditor, for *Hardening Cisco Routers*. Claire Cloutier, Tatiana Apandi Diaz, and Rachel Wheeler provided quality control. Johnna VanHoose Dinse wrote the index.

Emma Colby designed the cover of this book, based on a series design by Edie Freedman. The cover image is a 19th-century engraving from the Dover Pictorial Archive. Emma Colby produced the cover layout with QuarkXPress 4.1 using Adobe's ITC Garamond font.

Melanie Wang designed the interior layout, based on a series design by David Futato. Mihaela Maier converted the files from Microsoft Word to FrameMaker 5.5.6 using tools created by Mike Sierra. The text font is Linotype Birka; the heading font is Adobe Myriad Condensed; and the code font is LucasFont's TheSans Mono Condensed. The illustrations that appear in the book were produced by Robert Romano and Jessamyn Read using Macromedia FreeHand 9 and Adobe Photoshop 6. The tip and warning icons were drawn by Christopher Bing. This colophon was written by Ann Schirmer.